PORTRAIT

The emergence of John F. Kennedy

Bramhall House—New York

PORTRAIT
by Jacques Lowe

This edition published by Bramhall House, a division of Clarkson N. Potter, Inc.
by arrangement with the McGraw-Hill Book Company, Inc.
(A)

All photographs by Jacques Lowe, except family album pictures and those listed below.
Wide World: pages 9, 12, 17 (top and bottom), 18, 22, 24, 28, 29, and 30 (top and bottom).
Boston Globe: page 11. United Press International: pages 13, 16 (top and bottom), 31.

The author wishes to acknowledge his gratitude to Alan Levy for his assistance
in the preparation of the text, and to Compo Photocolor.

Library of Congress Catalog Card Number 61-17341

To Jamie and Victoria

The Fitzgeralds and the Kennedys

No man is a hero to his photographer—at least, so the saying goes among my colleagues. But my experience in the last few years has led me to doubt this truism.

While photographing John Fitzgerald Kennedy in the course of the Presidential campaign, and on many occasions before and since, I have had the opportunity to watch him closely. I have seen him in a variety of moods—equable and even-tempered, as he usually is, or fretting and fuming in situations that would try any man's patience. I have been compelled to criticize his sartorial taste (for photographic purposes), and I have squirmed while he wrote his name in blood at a Rotary Club lunch. I have also evolved from an unreconstructed Stevensonian to an ardent New Frontiersman—and perhaps even something of a hero-worshiper.

These experiences may be worth recording, not merely because the man I was photographing is now the President of the United States, but because they typify the ordeal that confronts any man today who yearns to change his address to 1600 Pennsylvania Avenue, Washington, D.C.

As a photographer I have tried to put JFK's life in the focus that one can possess only after working for him and with him. Perhaps it will be useful and of interest to see him as my camera and I have seen him.

A photo sometimes catches the lines in a man's face and telltale expressions more revealingly than the most detailed history books. And a photographer often becomes so interested in his subject that he delves into the man's past and even his ancestry.

Since JFK was born in New England a decade or so before I was born abroad, my knowledge of his early life is limited and indirect. It would be presumptuous to attempt in this brief space a biographical study, particularly since so many

full-dress biographies have already been published. But since 1957, when first I surveyed the crowded landscape of Kennedys, a project that seemed to require a CinemaScopic lens, I have read a great deal about the family and occasionally I've been present at a revealing moment.

Such a moment came one day in 1961 while I was photographing the President at the White House. He had begun to reminisce about a turbulent childhood summer on Cape Cod. Every summer that he has spent at Hyannis Port, Massachusetts, has been as noisy, exciting, and emotional as a political convention. Hot-weather reunions of the far-flung but always close-knit Kennedy family have always been dominated by swarms of children, punctuated by active projects in surf and sand, and invigorated by minor crises and instant solutions.

Yet no two summers were ever quite the same. The one that penetrated the White House in a shaft of nostalgia was the summer John Kennedy was twelve.

"That summer" said the President, "was the first time I *met* Bobby Kennedy. Of course, I had known him for three and a half years; after all, he was my brother." But not until he was forty-four months old did the aggressive and able Robert Francis Kennedy—now Attorney General of the United States—achieve a real identity in the mind of his handsome older brother. Yet the person who has encountered Bobby in recent years wonders how, even as an infant, he failed to make an immediate impression on anyone.

This may possibly be one key not only to what

John F. "Honey Fitz" Fitzgerald, John Kennedy's maternal grandfather and mayor of Boston, and James Curley, another mayor of Boston and political associate.

Ambassador Joseph P. and Mrs. Rose Kennedy,
John Kennedy's parents, at their summer home in Hyannis Port.

made Bobby run, not only to what made his brother John the country's Chief Executive, but also to why greatness has emerged from a wealthy family that could easily have parceled out its empire to its heirs and sheltered them from the hurly-burly of politics. Such aristocratic seclusion, however, was in neither the blood nor the bones of the President's parents, Joseph Patrick Kennedy and the former Rose Fitzgerald.

For John Kennedy, the second son, as well as for Bobby, the seventh of nine children, family life was the first political crucible. It was a struggle for emergence as an individual in a large group: each child strove for recognition, to merit the already-granted reward of dwelling in their distinguished father's glory. It was the kind of struggle that has more often than not ruined or scarred the lives of other sons of famous fathers. But within the Kennedy family it was a struggle governed by love and a thirst for amicable competition, never by rancor. Later, there would be battles in the outside world, but whether the enemy was a Japanese destroyer or the elusive specter of religious bigotry, the Kennedys have always drawn their serenity as well as their strength from their initial exposure in the family political arena.

Although John F. Kennedy's rise from riches to the White House is not in the classic pattern of the American political success story, the saga of his forebears did follow a traditional pattern. The President's ancestors were "bog," or "cottage," Irish. His great-grandfather fought for survival among the "shanty" Irish of Boston. His grandparents rose to the social level of "lace-curtain" Irish—a middle-class Bostonian attainment that has been characterized as "a family with fruit in the house when nobody is sick."

When the potato crop failed in Ireland in the 1840s and famine ensued, a wave of immigration washed to our shores, including among thousands of others the President's great-grandparents. Patrick Kennedy had left his thatch-roofed home and tiny farm in New Ross, County Wexford, raised the twenty-dollar steerage fare for an ocean crossing, and landed in Boston. About the same time and for the same reason, Rose Fitzgerald's grandfather, Tom Fitzgerald, left County Limerick and sailed from Cork to Boston.

Slightly more than a century ago, the Irish constituted the same "menace" to American society that the Puerto Ricans have been labeled in recent years. Historian James MacGregor Burns writes that Boston's immigrants lived high and low—in cellars flooded from backed-up drains; in garrets only three feet high—but invariably in poverty. When Pat Kennedy arrived in Boston, basements housed from five to thirty-nine persons each. By 1850, Irish paupers outnumbered Boston's total pauper population of all other nationalities combined.

Pat Kennedy found work as a cooper, making and mending the barrels that were rolled out in the more prosperous saloons. He married an Irish girl and they had four children. The first three were girls. Then Patrick J. Kennedy was born early in 1862.

The father died soon afterward, leaving the infant Patrick as the "man" of the house. Patrick's widowed mother took a job in a store and sent her son to a school taught by the Sisters of Notre Dame. When he was scarcely old enough to drink, young Patrick Kennedy opened a saloon near an East Boston shipyard. Kennedy's became

The house on Beals Street, Brookline, Massachusetts, where John Kennedy was born on May 29, 1917.

a popular tavern in shantytown—no noisy drunks allowed; no brawling on the premises; reasonable prices. His customers soon learned that this square-shaped little Irishman with handlebar mustaches could be a friend in distress. He readily helped out his fellow man once he became convinced that a tale of woe was more than malarkey.

By the turn of the century, Pat Kennedy owned several saloons, a liquor company, a coal company, and an interest in a bank. He had also become a Democratic ward leader in East Boston.

One of his political cronies was his future in-law, John F. Fitzgerald, better known as "Honey Fitz." A ward leader in the North End, Fitzgerald was a natural politician, red-faced, with sandy hair parted down the middle; his theme song was "Sweet Adeline." He could also render "Adelina Dulce" passably for an occasional Spanish-speaking constituent. The Boston *Herald* once remarked that "Honey Fitz" was the only man who could sing "Sweet Adeline" sober and get away with it But he went on to even greater fame as mayor of Boston—the first mayor, if James M. Curley can be trusted as a Boston historian, who possessed neither beard nor mustache.

"Honey Fitz" had a daughter named Rose who, when she was attending Dorchester High School early in this century, began "keeping company" with Patrick Kennedy's son, Joe, a senior at Boston Latin School. Their courtship lasted seven years, which spanned the young man's career at Harvard and his early days in banking. In 1914, when he was twenty-five, Joe became president of a Boston bank (making him the youngest bank chief in his state and possibly in the whole country) and married Rose Fitzgerald.

Joe Kennedy had gone into banking because he wanted to start at the bottom of a ladder that had more than one rung. He had begun by passing a civil-service examination and going to work for the state of Massachusetts as a $1500-a-year bank examiner. To gain control and the presidency of the Columbia Trust Company (the bank in which his father owned an interest), he had gone $45,000 into debt. But he bought the bank stock just in time to prevent a rival savings bank from gobbling up the Columbia Trust. He

borrowed another $2000 for a down payment on a three-story, $6500 house on Beals Street in suburban Brookline. Like many another young husband, bank president Joseph Kennedy began his married life deep in debt. But he didn't plan to stay in the red very long. He had vowed to make his first million before turning thirty-five—which would be in 1923.

As America's entry into World War I approached, Joe Kennedy turned the bank's management over to his father and became assistant general manager of the Bethlehem Steel shipyards in Quincy, Massachusetts. According to biographer Joe McCarthy, one of Kennedy's first observations was that there were few eating facilities for the shipyard's 22,000 workers, so he opened a cafeteria as a profitable sideline.

On the job with Bethlehem Steel, he frequently had to negotiate with government representatives. Perhaps his most formidable adversary in the battles of wits that preceded government contracts was Assistant Secretary of the Navy Franklin Delano Roosevelt. Kennedy and Roosevelt acquired the mutual respect that comes from frequent fights well fought.

After the war, Kennedy resumed his interrupted career as a financier. He studied the Yankee bigwigs so closely that he even took a Boston-to-New York train ride just to observe Galen Stone, a Boston investment banker, in action. This too was a profitable trip; soon thereafter Stone hired the ambitious young Irishman to head Hayden, Stone and Company.

Joseph Patrick Kennedy went on to become one of the legendary speculators of the 1920s. "He moved," said *Fortune* magazine later, "in the intense, secretive circles of operators in the wildest stock market in history—with routine plots and pools, inside information and wild guesses.... The legend of Joe Kennedy made him at once the hero of a Frank Merriwell captain-of-the-nine adventure, a Horatio Alger success story, an E. Phillips Oppenheim tale of intrigue, and a John Dos Passos disillusioning report on the search for the big money. The truth makes him the central character of a picaresque novel of a sort not yet written."

He moved vigorously on Wall Street and achieved renown as a fearless, tireless troubleshooter. Called in to save John Hertz' Yellow Cab Company from a stock crisis, Kennedy—ill with neuritis—got out of bed. He went to the old Waldorf Astoria Hotel, where he had his room equipped with wires and a ticker-tape machine. Too sick to stay on his feet, he climbed back into bed, and from his sickbed went to work on the telephones. When Hertz came to see him, Kennedy said that he would need five million dollars immediately to save the cab company. Hertz succeeded in raising the money in Chicago, with the help of his friends Albert Lasker and Phil Wrigley.

In a few weeks, Kennedy managed to halt the decline in Yellow Cab's stock. Hertz' five million dollars also was intact. This rescue operation exhausted Kennedy, who recalls that he did not stir from his hotel room for seven weeks.

Later, he bought a chain of New England movie houses and took over Film Booking Offices of America, both a booking agency and a Hollywood production company. He put this company on a paying basis by switching from lavish spectaculars to low-cost Westerns, which F.B.O. turned out at the rate of one a week. In Hollywood the Boston banker became chairman of Pathé, another film company, and won control of the Keith Albee Orpheum organization. He also found time for independent production. With Gloria Swanson as his star, he embarked on a series of movie epics.

Queen Kelly, starring Gloria Swanson, directed by Erich von Stroheim and produced by Joseph P. Kennedy, still stands as one of Hollywood's biggest disasters. In it Miss Swanson played the role of notorious Kitty Kelly. When *Queen Kelly* had been partly filmed, Kennedy fired the temperamental von Stroheim, but was unable to find a suitable ending for the sequences already on hand. *Queen Kelly* was shelved—at a loss of almost a million dollars. But Joe Kennedy recouped on another Swanson film, *The Trespasser.* Late in the 1920s he retired from Hollywood five million dollars ahead.

Even the stock-market crash did not affect Joe Kennedy drastically, although it had its emotional and political impact. Long before the Depression he had set up a million-dollar trust fund for each of his children. The crash shook his faith in the ultimate security of these funds and of our economic system in general. Aware that radical changes were necessary, he became

Next page: *The entire Kennedy family in four portraits taken between 1933 and 1940 in Bronxville* (upper right), *on the French Riviera* (lower right), *and in other places. From left are, seated* (in upper right picture, which includes all children), *Eunice, Jean, Edward (Teddy), on lap of his father Joseph P. Kennedy, Patricia, and Kathleen. Standing: Rosemary, Robert, John F. Kennedy, Mrs. Rose Kennedy, and Joseph, Jr. Joseph died as a Navy pilot during World War II, and Kathleen was killed in an airplane crash in France.*

15

an ardent backer of Roosevelt and the New Deal in 1932, and contributed handsomely to Democratic campaign funds. During the Depression days, through shrewd speculation, liquor-importing, and real estate, Kennedy continued to make money. He was seldom more than a few paces away from a stock ticker.

Throughout these adventures on both coasts, Joseph Kennedy never neglected his wife Rose, or their home. Their first child, born within a year of their marriage, was a boy; they named him Joseph, Jr. Their second child, also a boy, was born May 29, 1917, in the house on Beals Street in Brookline. They named him John Fitzgerald Kennedy.

There were seven more children—five girls and two boys. Joseph Kennedy, Sr., didn't seal any of them off from the world, even at their summer retreat in Hyannis Port. He trained his children to ask themselves two questions: "What shall I do about this problem?" and "What will Dad say about my solution?" At dinner, he discussed American government and politics and any other subject that was raised—except finance.

By virtue of seniority, Joe, Jr., and his brother John were the leaders. I caught a glimpse of them in a 1927 photograph, taken with nineteen other members of the football team at Dexter School, a private elementary school they attended in Brookline. Amid the prevailing blandness, Joe and Jack stand out in the crowd because of the determination they register even in a posed photo. Six years later, in similar photos, the John F. Kennedy we know today is clearly discernible. He is in football uniform again, wearing the colors of the Choate School in Wallingford, Connecticut. He played left end and tackle. A teammate recalls that he was "a tiger on defense."

One of the teen-aged John Kennedy's classmates at Choate, K. Le Moyne Billings, has said that he remembers the future President this way: "In prep school, you're not concerned about whether you or your friends will end up as big

John F. Kennedy at Dexter School in Brookline, complete with football helmet. The year was 1927.

businessmen, leaders of industry, great writers, or anything else like that. You just think of them as pals. But I always knew that Jack would have a good career. I knew he had a pile of dough, even if he didn't act as if he had the faintest idea of this. He kind of wanted to be a lawyer and he kind of wanted to be a journalist; but whatever he decided to be, I could tell that he would be successful at it. Of our whole class, he probably read more books and magazines and current-events publications—anything he could get his hands on—than anyone else did."

If John F. Kennedy's classmates at Choate didn't give much thought to the future, they nevertheless were good prophets. They were among the first to elect JFK: they voted him Most Likely to Succeed.

In his first try at college life, he did not live up to his classmates' accolade. Despite his football prowess, he was a frail youth, and soon after entering Princeton University in the fall of 1935, he fell ill. By the time he had recovered, he was far behind the other freshmen.

Yet, his choice of college showed the workings of an independent mind. His father, an old Harvard man, had wanted Jack to attend his alma mater, but because Jack's prep-school friends were going to Princeton, that's where he wanted to go too. A family friend has said that Jack got his way after a great many long "discussions."

Since even the proverbial old college try could not have salvaged his freshman year at Princeton, his father suggested that he spend the rest of it abroad, taking courses with Harold Laski at the London School of Economics. Joe, Jr., had also studied under Laski. This exposure of his sons to hostile viewpoints (Laski was a Socialist economist) seemed out of character for a tycoon like Joseph P. Kennedy, Sr., who by then had risen high in the investment-banking world and had served as chairman of the Securities Exchange Commission. But he believed that his sons should have contact with the best minds and most divergent viewpoints of their time.

Jack Kennedy returned from London and began college again—this time as a Harvard freshman, in September 1936. His health held up far better than it had at Princeton. He played hockey, rugby, and some football, but his forte was swimming—until he attempted to qualify for the Harvard-Yale meet by stealing away

from his sick bed while running a fever. Despite this setback, he remained active on the campus at Cambridge, majored in Government, and was graduated with honors in 1940.

During most of his undergraduate career, JFK's father was President Roosevelt's Ambassador to the Court of St. James's. Between college sessions and whenever he was needed, Jack Kennedy journeyed to London and assisted his father in the Embassy. England was already at war with Germany—but America was not—and the Ambassador's job was as dangerous as it was diplomatic.

When the British liner *Athenia,* with 300 Americans aboard, was torpedoed by a German submarine near Glasgow, Ambassador Kennedy dispatched his son to interview the American survivors, who wanted Navy protection for their next homeward try. Because the Ambassador could not offer them a convoy without endangering American neutrality, his son was met with a barrage of anger. "We've got six million dollars worth of United States Navy and they won't do this for us!" protested one angry American. Despite the highly emotional atmosphere, Jack Kennedy was able to piece together the key facts of the case.

During his father's stay abroad, Jack Kennedy traveled extensively in a Europe whose greatest single reality was Adolf Hitler. He visited Paris, Latvia, Russia, Turkey, Palestine, and Berlin—filing on-the-spot reports to his father's Embassy in Grosvenor Square.

While observing the present, he was also applying the lessons of the past and displaying an aptitude for putting knowledge to practical use. At Harvard, he had approached politics by chronicling the career of an unsuccessful New York politician and analyzing the mistakes that had made this man a party hack rather than an office-holder—mistakes that John Kennedy would try not to make. Similarly, he could see the European crises in historic perspective. Neville Chamberlain, noted for his desperate stab for "peace in our time" at Munich, was the cur-

John F. Kennedy toured Europe and the Near East just before the outbreak of war. Here he is in the Near East and Turkey.

rent scapegoat, but John Kennedy concluded: "Most of the critics have been firing at the wrong time. The Munich Pact itself should not be the object of criticism but rather the underlying factors, such as the state of British opinion and the condition of Britain's armaments, which made 'surrender' [at Munich] inevitable."

Not only did Jack Kennedy submit his study of appeasement as an honors thesis in political science; he also adapted it into a book, *Why England Slept,* which was published in the summer of 1940 while Hitler was overrunning Europe and massing his resources for the blitz of Britain. Timely and pungent, it became a best-seller.

At twenty-three, the Ambassador's second son was a successful author and a budding political philosopher. *Why England Slept* closed on this note, which also reflected the view of the author's father:

> To say that democracy has been awakened by the events of the last few weeks is not enough. Any person will awaken when the house is burning down. What we need is an armed guard that will wake up when the fire first starts or, better yet, one that will not permit a fire to start at all.
>
> We should profit by the lesson of England and make our democracy work. We must make it work right now. Any system of government will work when everything is going well. It is the system that functions in the pinches that survives.

The author's father was speaking more bluntly to the press. Joseph P. Kennedy's utterances at the time have led many to depict him as an isolationist, an appeaser, even an America-Firster. Such quotes as "I do not want to see this country go to war under any conditions whatsoever unless we are attacked" and "England is not fighting our battle. This is not our war" have been used against him. It must be remembered that he termed the Nazis antagonistic "to law, to family life, even to religion itself." James Mac-Gregor Burns has described Kennedy's position: "He simply refused to make a final commitment at a time when the world was choosing up sides— We or They.

And when England's battle became our own, the Kennedys responded. Young Joe joined the Navy and won his pilot's wings. It was more dif-

Upper picture: *JFK in Holland.*
Lower picture: *JFK in Egypt.*

When the liner Athenia *was sunk by German submarines off Glasgow, Scotland, John Kennedy, representing his father, together with U.S. Consul General Leslie Davis interviewed American survivors. The date was September 7, 1939. The United States was not yet at war with Germany.*

ficult for his kid brother Jack to get into the service. A spinal injury, suffered while playing football, kept him out of the Army and the Navy until he undertook special exercises and treatments to strengthen his back. Then he applied for a Navy commission and was accepted.

Paul Fay, Jr., now Under-Secretary of the Navy, recalls the deceptively youthful Lieutenant Kennedy at a torpedo-boat training station in Rhode Island. "The first thing I did," Fay is quoted in *The Remarkable Kennedys* by Joe McCarthy, "was to dig up a football and round up a bunch of the new guys who came there with me for a game of touch. We started to play and this skinny kid in a Harvard football sweater came walking down to the field and watched us. He asked if he could get into the game. I said sure, if he got another guy for the other team, which he did in a few minutes. Well, he wasn't in the game five minutes before he started arguing with me about the rules. I wanted to brain him. I figured he was one of the officers' kids.

"Well, the next day we started classes on how to operate the boats and it turns out that this same skinny kid is our instructor."

The "skinny kid"—some of his men referred to him affectionately as "Shafty"—could do it as well as teach it. On the night of August 2, 1943, Lieutenant (j.g.) Kennedy was the skipper of PT–109, patrolling the Blacklett Strait in the Solomon Islands.

Suddenly the lookout in the starboard gun turret shouted, "Ship at two o'clock!"

A Japanese destroyer, sleek and fast and gigantic, was bearing down on the tiny PT boat.

The destroyer hit them "like the *Queen Mary*," PT–109's radioman has recalled. Kennedy was slammed down on his back, and the radioman went down with him. Kennedy's own thought was: "This is how it feels to be killed."

The PT boat snapped in two. A gunner was swept into the sea and under the destroyer's propellers. Another gunner also was swept down. The little boat's fuel tanks, loaded with high-octane aviation gasoline, exploded in a blaze that convinced the enemy there would be no survivors.

There were, however. Ten life-jacketed Americans floated, in various degrees of shock and pain, in the oily waters. One engineer had landed in the flames and had been burned black. Another was half dead from swallowing gasoline. Kennedy dragged the burned man to a floating chunk of wreckage. Then he went back to help gunner's mate Charles Harris, a Bostonian whose left leg had been immobilized, and urged Harris to swim for the floating wreckage.

When the mate protested that he couldn't swim, Kennedy said, "For a man from Boston, you're really putting on some exhibition out here, Harris." But seeing that Harris' distress was genuine, Kennedy towed him to the remains of PT–109, which kept drifting away. It took them an hour to reach it.

The ten survivors were adrift in enemy territory with no food, drinking water, or supplies. The nearest island was a mile away. But on it, they believed, was a Japanese camp with men and trucks. The current was dragging them to-

23

Joseph, Jr., JFK's older brother, as a Navy pilot. On a dangerous volunteer mission over Belgium, his plane, full of explosives, blew up in the air.

ward it. When the wreckage they were riding began to founder, Kennedy pointed to an island some three miles away and told his men to swim for it.

He said that he would take the engineer, who was barely conscious. Tying the straps of the man's kapok life preserver together, Kennedy gripped them between his teeth and began swimming with the man in tow.

For five hours Kennedy tugged the survivor. "I couldn't believe the skinny kid would get very far with me," Pat MacMahon, the engineer, has recalled. "I knew he was in no great shape himself; he had been bounced down bad by the ramming. And he never looked more than a hundred-forty pounds to me, even on a good day, and today was not a good day."

Finally Kennedy told MacMahon, "Pappy, we're going in." He carried the engineer over a bed of sharp coral and both collapsed on the sand of the tiny atoll.

The others made it too, but their skipper didn't linger. He hitched up his shorts, walked into the sea, and swam slowly toward a point, several miles away, where American PT boats were likely to be patrolling. There he waited, treading water and signaling for help with a lantern he had salvaged from PT–109. Twelve hours later, he returned—feverish but not delirious—and passed out on the island.

That night he and his men swam a mile to another island closer to the patrol route. Again, Kennedy transported MacMahon with strong swimming and clenched teeth. Eventually they made contact with friendly natives, and then with a New Zealand infantry patrol operating on a nearby island. When a PT boat came for them on the sixth day, Lieutenant Kennedy said cheerfully, "Where the hell have you been?"

For his exploit he received the Purple Heart and the Navy and Marine Corps Medal. The citation read in part, "His courage, endurance and excellent leadership contributed to the saving of several lives and was in keeping with the highest

John F. Kennedy in the Navy.

tradition of the United States Naval Service." He had also received a further back injury that was to plague him for years.

Back home his family heard about his rescue with untold relief. But death was hovering close to the Kennedys. Jack's survival was only a reprieve. On August 2, 1944, exactly a year after his boat went down, two priests called on Joseph P. Kennedy, Sr., in Hyannis Port. The news was that Joe, Jr., had volunteered for a dangerous air mission over the Belgian coast. His plane, heavily packed with explosives, had blown up in midair. Joe's body was never recovered. "Your boy," Navy Secretary James V. Forrestal told Joseph Kennedy, Sr., "was unusual in every respect. He had guts and character and an extraordinary personality." The Navy named a destroyer *Joseph P. Kennedy, Jr.*

A month later, Joseph Kennedy, Sr., lost his son-in-law, the Marquess of Hartington. Kathleen Kennedy, three years younger than her brother Jack, had married the British peer while she was working abroad for the Red Cross. Kathleen's marriage had provoked consternation in Catholic Boston as well as in the Marquess' Protestant family. "One of England's oldest and loftiest family trees swayed perceptibly," a London newsman reported. But the newlyweds had only a few weeks together. The Marquess, a captain in the Coldstream Guards, was killed in action while leading an infantry patrol in Normandy. A fellow officer reported his last glimpse of the Marquess alive: "Billy Hartington was completely calm and casual, carrying his cap and saying rather languidly to his men, 'Come on, you fellows. Buck up.'" (Kathleen later died in France, in a 1948 plane crash.)

The war had taken its toll of the Kennedy family. Joe, Jr., had been an affable, natural politician, disarmingly frank in confessing his ambition: to be President of the United States. Now Joe was dead. The Kennedys' mantle of leadership had passed to the second son, John Fitzgerald Kennedy.

*The famous rocking chair.
Senator Kennedy relaxes
in his Senate office, in 1959.*

The political beginnings

Joseph P. Kennedy, Jr., had once said that when he was ready to start his ascent to the Presidency, he would begin in the Eleventh Massachusetts Congressional District, where his family had its roots. The Eleventh included East Boston, Ambassador Kennedy's birthplace, and the North End, birthplace of "Honey Fitz" and his daughter Rose.

Early in 1946, the Eleventh's congressman, James Michael Curley, vacated his House seat to resume the more familiar role of mayor of Boston. And John F. Kennedy, the twenty-eight-year-old hero and successful author, announced that he would seek "The Purple Shamrock's" niche in Washington.

On his first plunge into politics, Jack Kennedy was shy and diffident. He wasn't sure that he could charm the residents of the Eleventh or explain the issues to them, but he knew that if he worked at it, he could shake more hands than any other candidate in the district ever had. He also went from pub to pub asking who was the man that knew most about the district. Everyone agreed it was Dave Powers. Powers, now a special assistant to the President and a close friend, recalls their first meeting, when "the door bell rang and this young kid, very serious, came up and said, I am John Kennedy and I am running for Congress and I would like you to help me in this campaign." Dave laughed at this ingenuous approach, then invited him in. He listened to Kennedy's story and agreed to help. "There wasn't a wake, a wedding or a childbirth we didn't visit, a hand we didn't shake, or a name we didn't remember," Dave has said.

But Jack Kennedy had other help too. Not

The young campaigner, 1946. He won.

only did his family rally round its flagbearer; friends from school, college, and the Navy descended on Boston to join the cause. "Lem" Billings, his onetime roommate at Choate and Princeton, worked so avidly for Kennedy that the campaign was almost over before he realized his ludicrous casting: "Here I was a Republican working for a Democrat, an Episcopalian working in a Catholic district, a Pittsburgher working in Boston." But he worked harder than ever. Bobby Kennedy, who had quit school at nineteen to serve as a seaman on the destroyer *Joseph P. Kennedy, Jr.,* was discharged from the Navy just in time to join his brother Jack's troops. Bobby took charge of several East Cambridge wards.

The 1946 primary was one of those wide-open elections upon which Bostonians dote. Jack Kennedy's nine opponents for the Curley seat were a former mayor of Boston, a former secretary of Curley's, a Yankee, four Italians (two with the same name, Joseph Russo), a schoolteacher, and a WAC major. "Poor little rich kid," one of the old political pros sneered at first. But as the skinny youth began to run away from them, their jeers turned to howls of rage. With the money Joe Kennedy was spending on his son, the family chauffeur could be elected to Congress, the opposition insisted. They even charged (incorrectly) that Kathleen Kennedy's late husband had been a descendant of Oliver Cromwell, a name not calculated to win friends among Boston's Irish.

By then, Jack Kennedy had warmed to the fight. His strength mounted, but he continued to summon all his resources—particularly his family. Former Ambassador Kennedy and his wife Rose were guests of honor at a tea party for some 2000 women voters, who came to hobnob with the celebrated couple and left singing the praises of the Kennedys' son Jack.

28

John F. Kennedy, twenty-nine, casts his vote on June 18, 1946. He is flanked by his grandparents, Mr. and Mrs. John F. Fitzgerald. Kennedy won in a field of nine.

Upper picture: *JFK campaigning for Senate, 1952.*

Lower picture: *At Democratic national convention Kennedy almost receives Vice-Presidential nomination. On his right, National Chairman Paul Butler. The year, 1956.*

Victory in the June primary would be assurance of election. On primary day, John F. Kennedy—running in a ten-candidate race—received 42 per cent of the vote, defeating the nearest contender by almost two to one.

At the victory celebration, "Honey Fitz," then in his eighties, climbed atop a table, danced an Irish jig, and sang "Sweet Adeline." But Fitzgerald's performance was nostalgic as well as joyous. His grandson was going to Washington, where the ways of the Irish ward politician would be replaced by the ways of the statesman.

One of Representative Kennedy's first acts as a freshman in Congress was distinctly contrary to Irish political tradition. His onetime predecessor, James Curley, was in federal prison serving time for fraud. The Massachusetts Democrats in Congress were petitioning for Curley's release because "The Purple Shamrock" was not in the pink of health. Kennedy checked on Curley's condition and decided that the mayor of Boston (Curley retained his office while sojourning in the penitentiary) was not sick enough to warrant a Presidential pardon. His refusal to sign for a fellow Irishman was considered sacrilegious in Boston. Kennedy was the only dissenter among his state's Democratic delegation.

He began his office-holding life in the Eightieth Congress, a Republican-controlled legislature that earned the enduring scorn of the Democratic President, Harry S. Truman. It was not a happy hunting ground for a political liberal, but Kennedy was a practical man who concentrated on the few gains that appeared feasible. He fought for veteran's housing. As a war hero, he had considerable influence—on legislators and on the powerful veterans' lobbies that tended to oppose progressive legislation.

He managed to neutralize the Veterans of Foreign Wars in the housing battle, but it was harder to cope with the American Legion, which denounced the lanky, bushy-haired congressman as an "embryo." The debate continued, even after Republicans and Southern Democrats had thwarted the housing measures young Kennedy was seeking. One day he told the House of Representatives, "The leadership of the American Legion has not had a constructive thought for the benefit of this country since 1918!"

This was political suicide in the opinion of virtually every member of the House. Some members rose to defend the Legion's powerful brass against this scathing attack; others rushed to the impetuous congressman and urged him to retract. John Kennedy asked for the floor again, but he failed to "correct" his remarks; instead he denounced the Legion's leaders for opposing progressive housing measures.

"Well, Ted, we're gone!" Kennedy casually told an aide, Ted Reardon. But he had attacked the leadership, not the Legionnaires, and most of his mail was friendly. Even the attacks didn't bother him, for he had learned a valuable lesson in political courage. "The rockets go up and last for three or four weeks. Then people forget because they have so many problems of their own," he said.

He was not yet a national figure and he didn't make the freshman legislator's mistake of trying to behave like one. Instead, he looked after his constituents and tried to evaluate all bills from the viewpoint, "Is it good for the people of Boston?" He fought any legislation that conceivably could lure industry away from New England to the lower-cost Southland. And he sponsored federal aid to parochial schools, which won him new friends among his Catholic constituents.

"All you have talked about since you have been here is New England," one Midwestern congressman complained to him.

"Do you object to that?" Kennedy retorted.

One reason for the regional outlook of the young congressman, who occasionally was mistaken for a page boy, was his awareness that he had to learn the ropes before he could emerge as a statesman. He was developing a political philosophy, but until it had matured he was following the Kennedy tradition of being passionately committed to noncommitment—a policy that had harmed Joseph Kennedy, Sr., as Ambassador, but one that now did his son a world of good with the voters back home.

He was re-elected to the House with little difficulty in 1948 and 1950, but he was thinking ahead. As early as 1950, Kennedy aides began seeding the battleground of a 1952 campaign for the Senate. Two bright young men—Kenny O'Donnell and Larry O'Brien—formed Kennedy committees in some 350 Massachusetts communities and organized them into county and district groups. The task ahead of them seemed monumental, if not impossible. Kennedy's opponent would be Senator Henry Cabot Lodge, an impressive national figure with a good war record and plenty of voter appeal.

To make matters worse for an ambitious Democrat, 1952 was the year Dwight D. Eisenhower ran for President on the Republican ticket. And Lodge was no mere passenger on the general's coattails. He was Ike's campaign manager. Lodge seemed so formidable that the logical Democratic choice to oppose him, Governor Paul A. Dever, wasn't eager to risk it. He left the field wide open for Kennedy. Ironically enough, Dever, who played it safe by running for re-election as governor of Massachusetts, was defeated by Christian Herter. Part of his defeat was attributable to the television exposure he received when he was "showcased" as a principal speaker at the 1952 Democratic Convention and resembled, many thought, a cartoonist's version of an old-time politician.

Massachusetts' old-line politicians were not impressed either by the slender young man who had the gall to challenge Lodge. And they were rendered apoplectic by Jack Kennedy's choice of a campaign manager—his brother Bobby, fresh out of the University of Virginia Law School.

The female branch of the Kennedy family tree blossomed in 1952's heat of battle. Matriarch Rose Kennedy toured Italian wards, Irish wards, and even Yankee territory, chatting about clothes and children with other mothers. She showed her rapt audiences the card file she kept when her nine children were younger. It was a complete record of their past vaccinations and dentist visits—and when the next ones were due.

A series of Boston tea parties, followed by similar events across the state, were launched. That fall, housewives were astonished to open their mail and find formal invitations to come for tea or coffee and cookies with Rose Kennedy and her family. They came—as many as 2000 at a time. The candidate's sisters, Eunice, Pat, and Jean, were charming hostesses who made everybody feel wanted, even in a crowded hotel ballroom. True, after hearing some mercifully brief speeches, the guests might have to wait in line two hours to make small talk with the candidate's mother. But it was worth the inconvenience—and more than 50,000 Bay State women responded. For those who couldn't make it, the entire cast went on television in a hit show called "Coffee with the Kennedys."

Once, the campaign almost ran out of Kennedys. Somebody had overbooked the family, so Bobby had to rush into the breach and deliver a political address, quoted here in its entirety: "My brother Jack couldn't be here. My mother couldn't be here. My sister Eunice couldn't be here. My sister Pat couldn't be here. My sister Jean couldn't be here. But if my brother Jack were here, he'd tell you Lodge has a very bad voting record. Thank you."

On the first Tuesday after the first Monday in November 1952, a total of 1,211,984 votes were cast for John Fitzgerald Kennedy. Henry Cabot Lodge received 1,141,247: Kennedy won by 70,737 votes.

That same year, John Kennedy met a twenty-two-year-old socialite named Jacqueline Bouvier at a Washington dinner party. She was the daughter of John V. Bouvier, III, a Wall Street financier. Her mother, who had remarried, was now Mrs. Hugh D. Auchincloss. Jacqueline Bouvier had spent two years at Vassar and two years at the Sorbonne; now she was finishing her college life at George Washington University in the capital city.

The First Lady has described the early days of their romance in these terms: "It was a very spasmodic courtship. We didn't see each other for six months, because I went to Europe again and Jack began his summer and fall campaigning in Massachusetts. Then came six months when we were both back.... But it was still spasmodic because he spent half of each week in Massachusetts. He'd call me from some oyster bar up there, with a great clinking of coins, to ask me out to the movies the following Wednesday in Washington."

Having returned triumphantly to Washington in 1953 as one of the few Democrats to withstand —and even prosper—during the Eisenhower landslide, Jack Kennedy felt free to take time out to win Jacqueline Bouvier's hand. By then she was an inquiring photographer for the Washington *Times-Herald*. She has since described their subsequent courtship succinctly: After Jack was in the Senate, I began to see him, and then I began to see him more often, and after a few months we became engaged."

They were married on September 12, 1953, in Newport, Rhode Island, by Archbishop Richard Cushing of Boston. Bobby Kennedy was best man. There were 1200 invited guests plus 3000

gatecrashers, who broke through police lines and nearly crushed the bride. She did not appear pleased by the enthusiasm, but the groom displayed a politician's automatic response to a mob scene—he smiled benignly. Senator and Mrs. John F. Kennedy honeymooned in the Mexican beach resort of Acapulco.

The man who had removed Cabot Lodge from the Washington scene was automatically a celebrity. But in 1953 and 1954, the most notorious member of the Senate was Joseph McCarthy. As the Senate approached a showdown on the Wisconsin demagogue, Kennedy was nearing a crisis of his own. His back was acting up again and he was in almost constant pain. He took to crutches and his weight went down to a worrisome 140 pounds. On October 21, 1954, doctors at the Hospital for Special Surgery in New York attempted a lumbar spine operation, which was a failure. An infection set in and, while his wife and family prayed for him, last rites were administered. But the Senator rallied and soon was well enough to be flown on a stretcher to the Kennedys' winter home in Palm Beach for Christmas. In February 1955 he returned to New York, where the doctors attempted the operation again. This time they succeeded.

Recuperating in Palm Beach and anticipating a healthy future, John F. Kennedy once again drew on the past. He decided to write a book describing eight instances of political courage in American history. His heroes ranged from Senator Edmund Ross of Kansas—whose vote saved President Andrew Johnson from removal but killed his own bright political chances—to Senator Robert Taft, the Ohio conservative who spoke out against the Nuremberg trials. The Library of Congress' Legislative Reference Service sent him cartons of books. He also called in Ted Sorenson, his newly acquired legislative assistant, to do some of the legwork and help with the research. Out of this close partnership, with JFK in bed and Sorenson helping, grew a remarkable team that operated brilliantly during the campaign. Of course, the concept and writing were the Senator's. Jacqueline Kennedy also encouraged him, read to him, and took dictation. When *Profiles in Courage* was published in 1956, it began with a dedication, "To My Wife," and also contained this note: "This book would not have been possible without the encouragement, assistance and criticisms offered from the very beginning by my wife Jacqueline, whose help during all the days of my convalescence I cannot ever adequately acknowledge."

Profiles in Courage was an even greater success than *Why England Slept.* It received excellent reviews, including several on the front pages of the important literary supplements. Almost 180,000 hard-cover copies were sold in three years. (In 1960 and 1961, it reappeared on the best-seller lists.) Paperback sales totals run into seven figures. And far more significant than royalties or reviews to its author was one great honor that came in 1957: *Profiles in Courage* won the Pulitzer prize for biography.

Since Kennedy had been listed only as "absent by leave of the Senate because of illness" on December 2, 1954, when his colleagues had censured Joseph McCarthy by a vote of 67 to 22, the popular wisecrack soon after the author-Senator's return from Palm Beach was: "A little less profile and a little more courage, please."

Kennedy's failure to take a strong stand against the junior Senator from Wisconsin long haunted his political career. At a Gridiron Dinner in Washington reporters warbled, to the music of "My Darling Clementine":

> "Where were you, John?
> Where were you, John?
> When the Senate censured Joe?"

In 1956, however, John Kennedy had little enough time for the past. His health was restored and his future was bright. He was being talked up as a likely running mate for Adlai Stevenson. His chief assistant, Ted Sorensen, drew up a learned analysis that was released to influential Democrats. Sorensen had compiled statistics which "proved" that a Catholic Vice-Presidential nominee would actually gain votes for a Protestant Presidential candidate.

At the Democratic National Convention in Chicago, Kennedy placed Adlai E. Stevenson in nomination. Kennedy's speech—in which he said of Eisenhower and Richard Nixon, "One takes the high road and one takes the low road"—impressed both delegates and television viewers.

But Adlai Stevenson was not carried away. And, partly because Dwight Eisenhower's ill health had made the Vice-Presidential nomination a more vital political issue than ever, Stevenson told the convention:

After three months on crutches JFK enters New York's Hospital for Special Surgery, October 11, 1954.

The American people have the solemn obligation to consider with the utmost care who will be their President if the elected President is prevented by a higher will from serving a full term. . . . In these circumstances I have concluded to depart from the precedents of the past. I have decided that the selection of the vice-presidential nominee should be made through the free processes of this convention.

This was the signal for a free-for-all that involved Kennedy, Senator Estes Kefauver of Tennessee, Mayor Robert Wagner of New York, Senator Hubert Humphrey of Minnesota, and others. With less than twelve hours to go before the balloting began, Kennedy and his staff and his relatives began combing the city for delegates. They tracked them to Chicago hotels, night clubs, taverns, and to less reputable establishments.

Joseph Kennedy, who was in France, got on the transatlantic phone to boost his son's stock with the political leaders he knew. But Kefauver, having been Stevenson's chief Democratic adversary in 1952 and 1956, had a well-oiled machine working for him.

In the Chicago stockyards, where the convention was being held, Kefauver won 483½ votes on the first Vice-Presidential ballot and Kennedy 304. The other candidates attracted lighter support in what was basically a two-man struggle. On the second ballot, Sam Rayburn brought Texas into the Kennedy camp. Lyndon Johnson proclaimed: "Texas proudly casts its votes for the fighting sailor who wears the scars of battle."

Senator JFK receives visitors at Capitol Hill. An influential politician now, Kennedy is preparing to run for re-election and beyond that weighing the Presidential campaign. The year is 1958.

Jacqueline working with the Senator at his office.

Kennedy was hurtling toward the top. He led Kefauver, 618 to 551½, on the second ballot, only 68 votes away from the nomination.

But he had reached the peak of his strength. On the next ballot Kefauver went over the top. And Kennedy moved that the Senator from Tennessee be nominated unanimously by acclamation.

The Democrats suffered a debacle that fall, and Kennedy has since been grateful that Kefauver kept him off a losing ticket. In 1959 and 1960, while recruiting support for his Presidential-nomination drive, he always managed to charm Democrats who had supported Kefauver in 1956. He would greet them by thanking them for opposing him at the convention. Their wisdom, he implied, had kept him from political oblivion. This was also a subtle way of reminding these politicians that Adlai Stevenson was a two-time loser who would not make an attractive candidate in 1960.

A few days after the harrowing 1956 convention, Jacqueline Kennedy—seven months pregnant—had a miscarriage. But late in 1957 a daughter, Caroline, was born to the John Kennedys.

In the same year I entered the Kennedy family picture. But it was not the eminent Senator or his photogenic wife and daughter who were my first subjects.

Every magazine in the country seemed to want photos of Robert Kennedy, the dynamic new chief counsel of the Senate Select Committee on Improper Activity in Labor and Management. As a free-lance photographer, I became a commuter between my New York base and Washington. It got to be a standing joke between us. One day he would be expecting a photographer from *Redbook*—and it turned out to be Jacques Lowe. The next day I would be representing *The Sign*, a Catholic publication; and a few days later I would be photographing for *Collier's.* After a while he stopped asking me "How are you today?"; his query became "*Who* are you today?"

Robert Kennedy was particularly fond of my photo of his whole family, which ran in *The Sign*, and asked for twenty-four copies. The next time I saw him he invited me home to dinner. Soon after that he asked me to bring my two children,

Jamie and Victoria, for a week end at his home in McLean, Virginia.

Like millions of other Americans, my weekend hobby is photography. The Kennedys then had five children, who made excellent subjects. Robert Kennedy's home, Hickory Hill, was a paradise for city kids—complete with treehouses and tree ladders, swings, a swimming pool, a tennis court, and a menagerie of animal pets. "Daddy," Jamie announced profoundly, "There is more cookies and toys at the Kennedys than we have all year in New York."

Afterward, Bob Kennedy asked if he could see my pictures. I sent him the whole batch of contact prints and suggested that he mark those pictures which he liked best. When the contact sheets came back, he had "selected" 129 photographs.

I called him long distance to ask incredulously: "Do you know how many pictures you marked?"

"No, I don't," he replied, "but I knew there were a lot of them."

I gave him the statistic. "A hundred twenty-nine," he exclaimed. "That's a lot. Why don't you just take off a dozen or so?"

"Never mind," I said despairingly. "I'll do them all."

A week after I'd sent all 129 prints off to McLean, I received another request from Robert Kennedy: "I'd like another set of pictures. Dad's birthday is coming up soon and I want to give them to him as a present."

"You want *all* of them?" I asked.

"He'll love them," Robert Kennedy assured me. I headed for the darkroom.

Several weeks later, my phone rang shortly after midnight. The call came from Hyannis Port. "This is Joseph Kennedy calling.

"I want to thank you for a beautiful present. I think these are the most wonderful pictures I have ever seen. Would you be able to photograph the rest of my family?"

That flattering assignment proved to be the beginning of a two-year stint. It took me first to the family homes in Hyannis Port; through lonely vigils at Midwestern airports; into coal mines, hotel rooms, television studios, and the frenzy of a political convention. Ultimately, it resulted in several photo expeditions to the White House.

John Kennedy (second from left) runs gauntlet of business callers in corridor outside his Senate office.

The family today

The man who is now President of the United States is not merely a unique personality. He is the oldest surviving son of a dedicated family that is very closely integrated. They have always worked together for the success of each individual. When Kennedy tells the American people, "Ask not what your country can do for you —ask what you can do for your country," he is summoning our inner strength and calling for the sacrifices and stamina that one Kennedy can always expect from another.

In such a dynasty, John F. Kennedy has been "the chosen one" ever since his brother Joseph died in war. The family's directness and undisguised ambition has semi-medieval overtones; it reminds one of the European families in which the oldest son took over the family estate, the second son grew up to be a cardinal, and the third son a general. But in each case, whatever was accomplished represented a family effort. Americans often wonder whether this is good, but I believe that when such a family devotes itself to a high purpose, such as scholarship or public service, it can propel its members to impressive achievements. The Kennedy and Rockefeller families today and the Adams family in earlier days certainly exemplify this kind of accomplishment.

Nobody ever pointed his finger at John F. Kennedy and said, "Jack, you're going to be President of the United States." But when there was an opportunity for one member of the family to rise to the summit of public service, the rest of the family mobilized selflessly working toward this goal rather than going in individual direc-

tions. The success of one becomes the success of all.

"Do the Kennedys quarrel?" I have been asked.

"Not as far as I know."

There were a great many disagreements in the Presidential campaign, between younger and older brother, between son and father. However, once a decision was made, they united and moved in the same direction. No argument ever transcends the family's *esprit de corps*.

I remember that the customarily fearless Robert Kennedy did not think his brother should enter the Wisconsin primary early in 1960. Robert thought it was too dangerous. John Kennedy would be opposed by Hubert Humphrey from the adjoining state of Minnesota, who was well liked by his own constituents and had often been called the third senator from Wisconsin. Yet JFK felt that a defeat of Humphrey there would knock him permanently out of the race.

After Robert, by then his campaign manager, and several other advisers had warned him that he would be risking his political life there, JFK, backed by his father, decided to enter Wisconsin. He reasoned that he must run boldly and sidestep nothing if he was to overcome the Democratic Party's apathy toward him. He must take his case to the public—and win. If he came to

The entire Kennedy family today, in the Hyannis Port library of Ambassador Joseph P. Kennedy's house. Seated, from left: *Eunice Kennedy Shriver, Rose Kennedy, Ambassador Joseph P. Kennedy, Jacqueline Bouvier Kennedy, Edward (Ted) Kennedy, Sargent Shriver.* Standing, from left: *Ethel (Mrs. Robert) Skakel Kennedy, Stephen Smith, Jean Kennedy Smith, the President, Robert Kennedy, Patricia Kennedy Lawford, Joan (Mrs. Edward) Bennet Kennedy, Peter Lawford.*

the convention with a victorious record in every major primary, he would have a fighting chance. Anything less—even one defeat—would eliminate him. A ducked primary would revive the "all profile and no courage" whispers.

From the moment he made up his mind there was no dissent. Robert and his staff planted both feet firmly on Wisconsin soil and in a few grueling weeks managed to change an indifferent, sometimes hostile territory into a pro-Kennedy state. And Wisconsin became his first major victory.

In an era of oversold "togetherness," the family truly stands united. Their unity extends to political teamwork, touch football, and the way they spend their summers on Cape Cod in three houses surrounding a common triangular lawn. Each branch may have its own vocation, its own friends, and its own interests, but the family call is placed above all else. Whenever a Kennedy is needed by another Kennedy, he will be there.

When and if Robert or Ted Kennedy should run for the Senate or another elective office, rest assured that every member of the family will work just as hard for him as they did for his older brother. This is a contagious spirit that instantly affects the people who marry into the family. Ethel Kennedy, Bobby's wife, and Joan, who married young Edward ("Teddy") Kennedy, work tirelessly. Steve Smith, Jean Kennedy's husband, was a major force in the Presidential campaign. Eunice's husband, Sargent Shriver, performed yeoman's service. And Jacqueline Kennedy, as we shall see, worked hard in her husband's behalf until pregnancy retired her temporarily from the political scene. Those who marry into the family also join a big organization.

I am often reminded of the *New Yorker* cartoon during the campaign, showing two matrons in front of a television set, with figures scrambled on the screen. The first matron asks, "Which one is Kennedy," and the answer is, "I

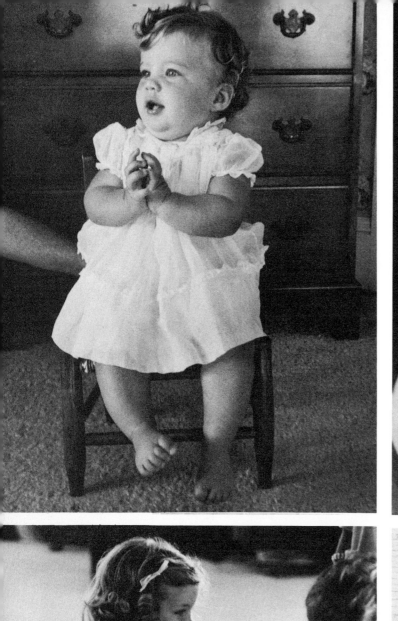

The back yard at 3505 N Street,
Washington, D.C.

think they are all Kennedys." This clan-likeness had its advantages during the campaign, when many spectators didn't quite know, just which Kennedy was addressing them. After Robert Kennedy appeared on the Jack Paar program, a survey showed that a great percentage of the viewers thought they had seen the Presidential candidate.

The inner circle of Kennedy advisers is always dotted with members of his family. They are always flexible; any friend of Jack's soon becomes a Kennedy-by-adoption. In the West Virginia primary there were more than forty key command posts—and to the best of my recollection, none of the commanders was paid. All were relatives or close friends upon whom the Senator could rely—talented, independent people who gave up everything for the cause. It was not uncommon to see a Wall Street broker, a solid Republican, working in West Virginia for the Democratic candidate.

There are many of these honorary Kennedys.

51

But now, let us take a look at the immediate family, their spouses, and some of their many children.

Joseph Kennedy is the patriarch. He is absolutely and undeniably the leader of the family. Though he purposely kept in the political background during the Presidential campaign, there is no doubt that as a father he was deeply involved in his son's aspirations. There was a constant and lively exchange of ideas between them, and often vigorous disagreements on basic ideas and tactics. Nevertheless, Jack Kennedy drew upon his father's strength and advice.

Now in his seventies, Joseph Kennedy still presents a picture of a vigorous, honest, straightforward man who looks young for his age. More than six feet tall, he has a lean, straight figure, silvery hair, and a high-colored complexion. His handshake is firm and his blue eyes behind horn-rimmed glasses have a friendly glance. He dresses meticulously and seems to take more interest in sartorial matters than does his son John. Age has not diminished his zest for life. To see him trying to embrace all his grandchildren in one large bear hug is to sense his enveloping affection for his family. He still rides horseback daily and often plays a round of golf when in the country, but he no longer participates in the rough and tumble of the famous touch football games.

Joseph Kennedy impressed me from the first as a very kind and warm human being. One incident will illustrate the fairness that this fabled businessman is noted for. I photographed a family wedding for Mr. Kennedy and, after I mailed him the prints he wrote me to say he was disappointed at the poor quality of the pictures, compared with my earlier work and the kind of creative photography he had expected. He also felt that in view of this my price was out of line. In a return letter, I agreed with his judgment, but pointed out the impossible job of shooting

Sailing with friend
Ben Bradlee in Nantucket Sound.

under conditions where I had no control over light or movement, a control essential for creative work. In an immediate reply Mr. Kennedy said that I had adequately justified myself and that he was perfectly satisfied. A check for the full amount was enclosed.

His wife, Rose Kennedy, is called "Mother" by every Kennedy, including in-laws. This small, slim (size ten) matron is a dynamic campaigner. One of my favorite stories about Rose Kennedy took place at the White House in the 1930s. Mrs. Joseph Kennedy went there to call on President Franklin D. Roosevelt. She was greeted by a White House aide who was so astonished to see that this famous mother of nine children was still a svelte, lovely woman that he remarked: "Well, Mrs. Kennedy, now I do believe in the stork."

An honor graduate of Dorchester High School at fifteen, Rose Fitzgerald attended Manhattanville College of the Sacred Heart and studied in The Netherlands before she married Joe Kennedy. Now in her seventies, she looks scarcely fifty. Even other women are quick to concede that she is a beauty. And a recent headline of a *McCall's* spread by Marguerite Higgins describes Rose Kennedy as "the family nerve center, linguist, politician, scholar and mother of nine. She wears a dress twenty years later—and looks sensational. And at seventy, she'd draw a second glance anywhere, even if her son weren't the President of the United States.

Rose Kennedy has become an expert on child-rearing. Her advice to mothers is quite simple. "You always take time to explain why you take a certain action," she has said. "You explain your attitude and you make it clear. This applies to big things. It applies as well to little things. ...If it was Thanksgiving, we would tell them why we ate turkey on Thanksgiving and why the Pilgrims set aside this day as a time of feasting and prayer. Then we would take them to Plymouth Rock to see where the Pilgrims landed."

During the Presidential campaign, the elder Kennedys would check with the candidate's en-

tourage nightly—but not with political advice; they knew he was getting plenty of that. They wanted to know whether the Senator was eating right, sleeping enough, and guarding his health. And did he have plenty of white shirts?

Rose Kennedy gazes on her son John's accomplishments with wonder. "We are so very proud," she has said, "and yet in some ways it seems unreal . . . him in his little sweater."

I first met John F. Kennedy himself a few weeks after the midnight call from his father. Joseph Kennedy telephoned again. His son, the Senator, was coming to Hyannis Port the following week. Could I come up then?

When I arrived at the "big house," Joseph Kennedy's home, I learned that the youthful Senator had gotten in at 4 a.m. from a thirteen-day trip. He would be taking off that night on another strenuous journey in preparation for his 1958 Senate re-election campaign. Surely during the few hours he would be spending with his family, the last man on earth whom he cared to

Mother and daughter spend a great deal of time together. Jacqueline Kennedy spends little time that doesn't include her daughter.

see was a photographer. Nevertheless, there I was!

My first impression was that he was rather distant and solemn. He was on the phone constantly, even while lunching on scrambled eggs; and he seemed far different from the more extroverted Bobby and his unassuming father. At this time I was still a confirmed Stevenson Democrat, and I found it easy not to like him too well. However, Jacqueline was cordial and hospitable, and pleased to have Caroline photographed. When we were ready to take pictures, JFK was very cooperative, and had an ease about him that regrettably he would never show again. When I compare the pictures showing the Senator relaxed and playing with Caroline with similar ones taken more recently, I can see the strain of his awesome office reflected in the new pictures.

After the sitting was over he thanked me in a rather distant manner. But when he saw the pictures, he was delighted. Recalling his mood at the time they were taken, he found it hard to believe that he had photographed so well. I received an enthusiastic note of congratulation from Jacqueline. And my brief contact with him snowballed into the job of official photographer for his Presidential campaign.

Robert Kennedy has long impressed me as the ideal American, the kind I read about as a boy in frontier tales and pioneer stories. At thirty-five he is the youngest Attorney General in this century, and already one of the ablest. He has a strong, muscular build, sandy, tousled hair, and penetrating blue eyes which can be steely in tough negotiation and warm and friendly with his family or associates. His relentless energy, while working a straight eighteen-hour day or playing a set of tennis with his wife before breakfast at eight, is astonishing. His habits are almost puritan; he doesn't smoke, drinks little, eats simply, and works hard—whether as chief counsel of the McClellan Committee, campaign manager for his brother, or as Attorney General of the United States.

His mind functions logically and directly, uncluttered by intellectual theorizing. He can tackle seemingly unsurmountable stumbling blocks and transform them into steppingstones.

I have had many occasions to observe him in action, both during the campaign and later as Attorney General. His brusque, seemingly cold manner has aroused some resentment. He sticks by a principle against all odds. But he can also be gentle and emotional. Anyone present at the time of Senator Humphrey's withdrawal from the Presidential race, after his decisive defeat in the West Virginia primary, saw a different Bobby Kennedy, as he turned to the Senator with tears in his eyes and put his arms around Humphrey's shoulders.

As a family man, the same principles apply. He is devoted to his wife, Ethel, and to their seven children. Life in their big, white-brick house in McLean is usually full and hectic. In addition to the family there are innumerable horses, dogs, cats, ponies, ducks, geese, rabbits, white mice, and anything else that will crawl; plus a variety of neighbors' children and friends of friends. When Robert Kennedy is at home with his children, he participates fully in their activities and initiates many of them.

Robert's wife, Ethel Kennedy, the former Ethel Scakel of Greenwich, Connecticut, is of course a great source of strength for her husband. An outgoing woman and an understanding wife, she never complained, despite Bobby's long absences from home during the campaign. She herself was a hard campaigner, and earlier, during the labor-rackets hearings, she could be observed daily, standing by her husband as chief counsel. She too seems to have inexhaustible energy. I remember seeing her play touch football in Hyannis Port one summer, when she was expecting another child. The next Sunday she was in the hospital, and when I saw her two months later in New York, she was as slim and attractive as ever.

Edward (Teddy) Kennedy is the youngest boy and the baby of the family. He is powerfully built, and almost as tall as the President, but he resembles Bobby most closely in appearance, behavior and manner. He works hard and plays hard with the usual Kennedy intensity. The clarion call among them is "Wait until you see what Teddy can do!"

Teddy graduated from Harvard with the class of '56 and then studied law at the University of Virginia. On November 29, 1958, he married Joan Bennet of Bronxville, New York, in a wedding to which one New York tabloid devoted its entire front page. Blonde, blue-eyed Joan has since become a full-fledged member of the clan. Today, the Edward Kennedys are the only family couple still living in their native Boston, where Teddy is an assistant district attorney.

Throughout the campaign, from their base in San Francisco, where her husband was coordinator of the thirteen Western states. Joan would trek across the country, joining her in-laws or going it alone in speeches before women's groups, teas, and other social gatherings, joining her husband whenever he managed to get back to San Francisco.

During the campaign Teddy was a perpetual friend in need to me. A campaign is an endless series of passes, credentials, and security checks. Whenever I got into trouble with a cop, usher, or other self-appointed guardian of a nonexistent law, Teddy was ready to help me out. Once,

when I battled desperately to get into the convention hall, Teddy spotted me, rushed over, and handed me his badge, only to have the guard snatch it away from me. Kennedy or no Kennedy, he declared, he was in charge of that door and would let no one through without the proper credentials. For a moment it looked as if even Teddy would not prevail, but finally the long arm of the law relented and let me in.

Eunice, the next daughter and John Kennedy's favorite sister, married Robert Sargent Shriver, who now heads his brother-in-law's imaginative program, the Peace Corps. Shriver is well qualified for this job. A Yale graduate and former editor of *Newsweek*, he has for years been concerned with social justice and interracial progress. An able businessman and assistant manager of the Merchandise Mart, he has frequently been mentioned as a potential governor of the State of Illinois.

As president of the Chicago Catholic Interracial Council he actively promoted interracial justice in such fields as housing, schooling, and employment. Some of his ideas in this field influenced action beyond the city of Chicago. As a member of the Illinois State Board of Education he was deeply concerned with the reading matter used in Illinois schools. He also worked with many interdenominational groups toward the betterment of community relations.

Eunice has been executive secretary of the Department of Justice's juvenile-delinquency section and a social-service worker for the House of the Good Shepherd. She studied social science at Stanford University and, at the close of World War II, handled for the State Department the reorientation program of American prisoners of war being returned from Germany. In earlier days at Hyannis Port, she used to take notes at the dinner table when any item of conversation seemed to be worth following up. Eunice still is the girl intellectual of the family.

Despite their exceedingly active lives and three children of their own, the Shrivers have found time to take in foster children for periods of a year or longer. Eunice and the other Kennedy women take an active interest in the Kennedy Foundation, formerly headed by R. Sargent Shriver, which has devoted many millions to research and practical help in the field of mental and physical retardation.

Robert F. Kennedy with his son Michael.

Patricia Kennedy is married to actor Peter Lawford. In general, the Lawfords are more removed from the political scene than any of the other family couples. But in 1956, when John Kennedy made his gallant bid for the Vice-Presidential nomination in Chicago, the Lawfords helped out from California.

Patricia and the British film actor met in 1953. When Peter proposed, Pat—in what sounds like a Hollywood plot—insisted on taking a trip around the world before making up her mind. She started out from San Francisco, got as far as Tokyo, changed her mind and returned to California. She married Lawford shortly afterward.

Joe Kennedy has been won over by his urbane theatrical son-in-law, despite an initial hostility. Earlier, Kennedy was quoted as telling Lawford bluntly: "If there's anything I think I'd hate as a son-in-law, it's an actor, and if there's anything I think I'd hate worse than an actor as a son-in-law, it's an English actor."

The Lawfords are active in California's Family Rosary Crusade, a drive to get families to pray together at least once a day. And Pat, while not the keen politician that other Kennedys are, did serve as a California delegate to the Democratic convention that chose her brother.

Jean, the youngest Kennedy sister, is married to Stephen Smith, heir to a New York barge and tugboat empire. Slight, retiring, dapper, and cordial, Steve was second only to Robert Kennedy in work performed during the campaign. Early in 1959 Steve set up the first Kennedy-for-President office, in the Esso building in Washington, a five-minute walk from the Senate. It was from there that the first strings were pulled together. Starting as the office manager, Steve eventually became administrative chief of the incredibly complex machinery that today is necessary to elect a President. He handled the preconvention campaign trips and later organized the corps of advance men who lined up each campaign ex-

pedition with uncanny precision. Steve is self-effacing, but he ranks as one of the people in whom John F. Kennedy places utmost trust. Steve is an ideal troubleshooter.

Jean is outgoing and sparkling. In Joseph Kennedy's files there is ample evidence of Jean's impishness. As a little girl, she sent her father a negative report on her big brother: "Jack was a very naughty boy when he was home. He kissed Betty Young under the mistletoe down in the front hall. He had a temperature of 102 one night, too, and Miss Cahill couldn't make him mind." She recommended a good spanking.

She has worked as an aide to Father James Keller, founder of the Christophers. And she has said, with a smile: "The trouble with being a Kennedy is that people always mix us up. Women are continually asking me how it feels to be married to Peter Lawford or if it's true that my husband may run for governor in Illinois."

Jacqueline Bouvier Kennedy, the First Lady and the most beautiful of the Kennedy women, stirs enthusiasm and draws great crowds whether she is in Washington or on state visits abroad. During the President's trip to Europe in June 1961 I saw a silent crowd outside the Vienna town hall waiting four hours just to catch a glimpse of Jacqueline. Quiet and somewhat withdrawn, she is perhaps the most introverted member of the Kennedy clan. She doesn't seem to enjoy the public spotlight—especially where it affects her two children, whom she is determined to keep unspoiled.

In order to understand her character one must know something about her background. The daughter of a socialite family, Mrs. Kennedy has the breeding and education of the true patrician, and was once voted debutante of the year. Her chief interests lie not in politics but in the arts. Her French descent and her studies at the Sorbonne in Paris have made her a Francophile, and her former home in Georgetown gave ample evidence of her taste in things French. During her

Ethel Kennedy reading to her children in Hyannis Port. From left: *Bobby, Joe, David, Mary Kerry, Kathleen, Michael, Courtney.*

*A day with the
Robert Kennedy family
at Cape Cod.*

husband's senatorial days she used to answer his French correspondence.

Mrs. Kennedy's Gallic interests really stem from a sense of the past, and here there is a strong link with her husband, for the President's sense of history shapes much of his thinking. She is also deeply interested in Americana and has been redecorating the White House with authentic period pieces and works of art. Her personal library of art books is enormous and she has collected master drawings for years. Raising and arranging flowers are also among her hobbies.

In the early days of her marriage, when her every move was something less than a national event, Jacqueline Kennedy used to make sure that her husband ate regularly and well. She would have her cook prepare a lunch and take it to the Senator's office at noontime. If the Senator was having guests, the cook in the Georgetown kitchen prepared a sumptuous repast, to be served at John Kennedy's desk, under the direct and dainty supervision of his wife.

Mrs. Kennedy appears sometimes less than delighted by the traffic congestion that now clutters her husband's life. There was one morning in Hyannis Port when he was holding a meeting with leaders of Hungarian, Polish, and Slovak societies. In the sitting room men were talking into several telephones—each in a different language. When the future First Lady came down for breakfast, she seemed bewildered by all that was going on. I asked her if there was anything I could do. "No," she replied. "I'm just trying to find a place to have breakfast. I'll try the porch." On the porch sat half a dozen Boston politicos and their wives, enveloped in cigar smoke, waiting to pay their respects. Jacqueline shook hands all around and tried the dining room next. Her husband was still in conference there and, when he saw her in the doorway, he waved his arms frantically. She quickly shut the door. The only place left was the kitchen; there she found Pierre Salinger holding a press conference, with some thirty reporters surrounding him.

This occurred in the summer of 1960, after her husband had won the Democratic nomination. Later that day I took pictures of her at her painting, which is disarmingly primitive in style. It is often topical, as illustrated by her painting welcoming her victorious husband back to Hyannis Port after the 1960 Convention.

Joan Kennedy plays piano for Jean and various Kennedy children.

But long before then it was apparent that she was awaiting the bright future with some trepidation. A few days before the convention we were both chatting in Hyannis Port. Jacqueline Kennedy said, "Oh, I hope Jack is going to get the nomination."

Mingled with her hope was a hint of fear too. "The way you say that," I remarked, "it sounds as if you don't want him to win the election. He's got to win the election. Nixon can't be President!"

"I know," she said. "But sometimes I am not thinking of the country. I am thinking of my own family."

Her relationship with her children, particularly with little Caroline, is very close. While Caroline considers her father something of a playmate— she calls him *Daddy,* he calls her *Buttons*—she regards her mother as a confidante. Mrs. Kennedy and Caroline go for long walks together, play together, and share secrets. Caroline is a happy, uncomplicated little girl who says, "Hi, what's your name?" to any stranger. Her mother will see to it that her infant brother, John F. Kennedy, Jr., who was born between the election and his father's inauguration, will grow up just as unspoiled.

In my professional relationship with the John Kennedys I have been very fortunate, for they both appreciate good camera work. Having been a photographer herself, Mrs. Kennedy is especially aware of the esthetics of photography. On occasion, when a picture that she didn't like has appeared in print, she has let me know. However, her appreciation, when she feels it is deserved, knows no bounds, and her husband can be equally enthusiastic.

In the summer the Kennedys all convene in Hyannis Port, where they fill three houses— Robert Kennedy's, JFK's, and "the big house," Joseph Kennedy's home, where the other families stay. The life is comfortable and informal. They raid each other's iceboxes. At three o'clock on any afternoon the Kennedys may not know which house will be serving dinner that night. Children dominate the proceedings at Hyannis

*Eunice Shriver with her daughter
Maria and son Robert.*

Port. They outnumber the adults. At press time, Bobby Kennedy had seven children—and the others have sizable delegations, too. Children tend to attract other children, so there are countless playmates, buddies, and "best friends" some of whom were met fifteen minutes ago. There are tennis courts, plenty of beach, and water, water everywhere. The Kennedys take boat rides to nearby islands, where they down picnic lunches—peanut-butter sandwiches and soft drinks, usually. There are no spectator sports, but complete participation.

On Sunday afternoons, Joseph Kennedy gets out his movie projector and shows films for the kiddies. Their cinematic taste ranges from Walt Disney to war movies. Speaking of pictures, the entire family is photo-crazy. The 129 photos I made for Bobby Kennedy are framed all around his walls. The big house in Hyannis Port is full of photographs, commemorating the families and the progress of the various children. An elegant Kennedy home often bears a startling resemblance to a barber shop in the theater district. Their Christmas cards are photographic. For birthdays, they give each other photos.

The Kennedys are always competing—with each other or against others. Sometimes, at Hyannis Port, it's a touch football game with the Kennedys versus the non-Kennedys (guests and other recruits). Then the voice of the Attorney General can be heard exhorting: "Okay, Kennedys! Let's go!" At other times, it's the boys against the girls.

I remember that one summer at Hyannis Port there were three broken arms in the family. The Kennedys play hard and nobody takes an injury very seriously. You break an arm. The doctor sets it. That's that. What do we do next? Even the youngest Kennedys are always looking forward to new frontiers.

Steve Smith and his son Stevie.

Quest for labor support.
Senator Kennedy addresses group of
labor executives in Los Angeles.

The primary trail

By July 1959, John F. Kennedy was looking toward January 20, 1961—the day he hoped to move from the Senate to the White House. It is a short trip that can be made comfortably in ten minutes. But it took him eighteen months and 400,000 miles of strenuous campaigning to get there.

Ever since the Democrats went down to defeat in 1956, potential candidates for President had been milling around the Capitol cloakrooms, listening for groundswells of popular support, and making known their availability. Senator Hubert Humphrey of Minnesota, Senator Stuart Symington of Missouri, and Senator Lyndon B. Johnson of Texas were frequently mentioned. Nobody was ruling out Adlai E. Stevenson from a third try. Governors "Pat" Brown of California, Robert Meyner of New Jersey, and "Happy" Chandler of Kentucky were taken less seriously. But Senator Kennedy was clearly the front-runner— and he was running hard.

None of the contenders would officially announce his candidacy until early 1960. To throw one's hat into the ring too early would be to risk being old hat by convention time. Nevertheless, by the summer of 1959 all the would-be Presidents were hard at work—even though, officially, they were still deciding—"undercover candidates" they might be called.

Steve Smith, JFK's brother-in-law, called and asked me to join the first unofficial campaign foray into Nebraska. I jumped at the chance and asked what kind of photos Senator Kennedy wanted.

"Well," Smith said, "let's just see what happens."

72

This portrait, taken at a news conference in Omaha, Nebraska, became the National Campaign poster.

It was in a mood of exhilaration that the Senator, his advisers Ted Sorensen and Hy Raskin, Steve Smith, and I boarded a rented plane at LaGuardia Airport at seven one morning. Everybody had the feeling of plunging in. And if we were lucky, we would be up to our necks in work until Election Night, 1960.

The event in Nebraska was a Democratic barbecue where people come ostensibly to roast chickens, but actually to look over and perhaps roast a candidate or two. We arrived at one in the afternoon and met with the Nebraska Democrats who were already for Kennedy. These were farmers and state senators and party workers— about thirty in all. JFK spoke briefly and gave his talk in matter-of-fact terms. Then his supporters asked such questions as "How are we going to organize?" and "What should we do first?"

Kennedy and his advisers had the answers. They told the Nebraskans what should be done and what should not be done; when they should start using posters and when they might begin an advertising campaign. It was my first glimpse of Kennedy politicking for the Presidency, and it was obvious that he had been giving this campaign plenty of careful thought.

Later that day the Senator faced the barbecue crowd and held a press conference.

At that time, Kennedy was a quiet young man who answered each question logically and calmly. He stood close to the microphone, and there was little movement and hardly any zip to his plat-

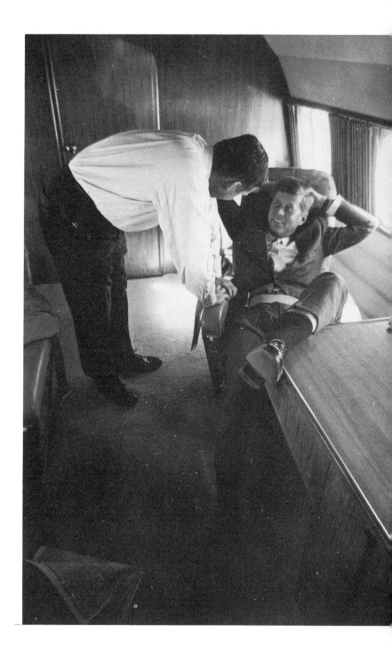

Aboard the "mother ship" Caroline. *Pierre Salinger at left.*

form performance. He seemed like an able junior executive who had been doing his homework, but not the kind of campaigner who would diminish my own zeal for Adlai Stevenson. His speech was eloquent when he quoted Robert Frost, but it didn't strike me as having any real guts. And there was little audience reaction.

If there was anything truly impressive about the Kennedy of the 1959 "undercover" campaign, it was this: *He never talked down to an audience.* If he was addressing a farm group, he didn't play the cornball or insert small-talk in his speech. He spoke about man's higher aspirations —simply and never too distantly. His listeners went away occasionally uplifted, occasionally unimpressed, but never patronized.

By September, the Kennedy campaign had a plane of its own. We rode in a leased Convair called the *Caroline.* It was our mainstay for a year, until Kennedy's press coverage and staff required several huge jets.

There are few lonelier ordeals than the pre-primary campaign of a Presidential hopeful. Remember those crowds that, in 1960, lined his route from each airport to the local hall? Less than a year earlier, in many of the same places, Kennedy would be met at the airport by a couple of local Democrats and, if he were lucky, a news reporter. It was considered an unusual event when, in Coos Bay, Oregon, he was met by a motorcade of a dozen cars. Sometimes he would have to linger at the airport while a poky local reception committee decided what it was going to do with him next. But this was exactly what he was there for—to spot the deadwood, weed it out, and build an efficient organization.

Kennedy is not a man who thrives on apathy, but he was comforted in those days by the almost constant presence of his wife. She presided at teas in Oregon and at farm-equipment auctions in the Midwest. Then her husband would say a few words. But at that time the Kennedys were seldom the stars—just the Extra Added Attractions.

Among politicians he was earnest and digni-fied. I remember a Democratic "show of unity" involving most of the contenders—and Harry S. Truman. The former President struck me that day as a man who liked to throw his weight around; he acted as if he were *the* kingmaker.

In the early days the Kennedys were met by only a few faithful partisans at the airport.

At Mills College, Oakland, California.

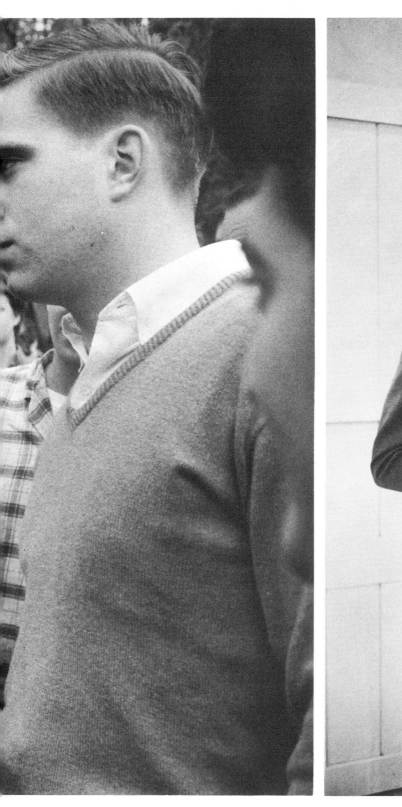

He treated all the candidates—even his friend Stuart Symington—as if they were striplings.

We went to California that fall. Frank Sinatra, Dean Martin, and Shirley MacLaine entertained at one Kennedy appearance. In one day we flew across the state, making eight stops, from Oakland to Los Angeles, ending up at Disneyland. When we got there, President Sekou Touré of Guinea was there with his State Department escort and his aides. Touré's official entourage and the accompanying press corps made up a larger party than our own small group. Right then and there, Kennedy, who was chairman of the Senate subcommittee on African affairs, had a meeting with President Touré.

Disneyland was one of our more enjoyable stops. I can't say the same for Kennedy's other adventures. Once he addressed a group of Rotarians who had dressed up as pirates. His speech, however, was a mere preliminary. Afterward, he was required to sign the register—in blood, *his own blood.* An old tradition, he was told. They took blood from his finger and then he signed his name. His wife was with him, and I think it actually hurt her more than it hurt him. She was aghast. It had never occurred to her that to get to be President her husband had to give blood to the Rotarians.

In general, the trip west was rewarding for Jacqueline Kennedy. At one point she met the chief of the Nez Perce Indians. He was apparently her first live Indian and she gazed at him with almost childlike wonder.

In those days she was not so besieged by photographers and interviewers as she is today. And when I asked her to pose in front of a sign for the Let 'Er Buck Motel, in Oregon, where the group spent a night, she good-naturedly complied. Throughout this tour she chatted easily about homemaking and children with newshens from the women's pages, and often presided at the famous Kennedy tea parties. She also signed a lot of autographs for the high school students who surrounded her after her husband's talks.

Kennedy often spoke at high schools, partly because his early "campaigning" was theoretically nonpolitical and mostly because he couldn't get other speaking dates. There wasn't a vote to be had among those kids, but when a candidate made a good impression on them, their parents were the first to hear about it.

As the campaign progressed things became far more difficult. Kennedy was starting to encounter resistance, and his audiences were beginning to ask him leading questions. "Senator Kennedy, would you explain to me: what is a Democrat?" asked one skeptical young lady with a deadpan expression. Kennedy fielded it adeptly. He cited the political differences between Thomas Jefferson and James Madison, and, without ever losing his audience's attention, gave the young woman a solid answer to a nebulous question. His familiarity with the past once again proved useful in the present.

I don't know how he kept up his reading, but he did. Of course, being a Senator requires rapid reading—of mail, newspapers, the *Congressional Record,* the political barometers. And perhaps a fast-reading course he once took helped, too. Anyway, his lively curiosity and well-disciplined mind kept him at it, even under the tremendous pressure of a campaign. On a radio interview, an announcer once made a slighting remark about Charles de Gaulle, whom Kennedy admires. The Senator rose to the general's defense in passionate and knowledgeable terms. He had read the latest installment of De Gaulle's memoirs—which had come out just three days earlier.

At a Far Western university, he quoted Euripides in his speech. Some professor there just couldn't resist trying to trip up a man who was running for President. The professor asked the speaker if he would please interpret the quote from Euripides. Kennedy obliged with a learned discussion that practically floored the professor. He sat down with his mouth wide open, gasping, "Thank you, Senator."

Kennedy was always well briefed by his aides (most of whom addressed him as "Senator," though a few old friends from prep school still called him "Jack") on the territory he was entering. On the plane he would read the local newspapers—in those days his name was on the inside pages—while downing his regular campaign diet of clam chowder, steak, and an occasional Heineken's beer. But equally important in those days was handshaking. As his campaign gathered momentum, endless lines of people filed by to meet Mr. and Mrs. Kennedy. His usual comment was a cordial "So glad you could come."

It was at a high school in Oregon that I first heard the religious issue aired. Working near the platform, I saw a commotion in one section of the audience. A few of the kids were jostling each other, apparently trying to work up the courage to ask a tough question. Finally, a boy in an athletic uniform with the number 35 stood up and said, "Senator Kennedy, can a Catholic become President?"

Kennedy didn't fall through the floor. He didn't even duck. Although the question was impersonal, the answer wasn't. He replied that the Presidential oath is similar to the oaths that he took upon entering the Navy, the House, and the Senate. If he had proved capable of fulfilling those oaths, there was no reason why he couldn't fulfill the Presidential vows. Then he affirmed his faith in the separation of church and state, throwing in another history lesson while answering the lad's question. He also pointed out that nobody had asked his brother Joe if he had divided loyalties before he could be permitted to die for his country. The audience applauded.

In the closing days of 1959, we were picking up crowds, but there were still some terrifying lonely moments. In Oregon, Kennedy walked into a union hall to find eleven men waiting to hear him. Without hesitation he launched into his speech.

But the politicians were starting to seek him out. Early in the year the Kennedy staff—consisting in those days of Robert Kennedy, Ted Sorensen, Larry O'Brien, Kenny O'Donnell, Steve Smith, and Pierre Salinger—with the help of pollster Lou Harris had set up grass-roots organizations of their own. Now, as these groups grew, many local politicos wanted to join in, and a great many meetings reminiscent of those in "smoke-filled rooms" began to take place. The smoke-filled rooms were often in airport motels, where a quick conference could be held and the Senator could promptly return to his plane.

I became conscious of other political problems as our swing continued. Not all the tea parties with Mrs. Kennedy were having the desired effect. Many of the old ladies who conducted them in small towns were lifelong Republicans who intended to stay that way. They had obtained their assignments because (1) they considered themselves the only people in town on a high enough social plane to associate with the Kennedys, and (2) many of the Democratic women had jobs and were working at three-thirty in the afternoon or whenever a tea party was scheduled. The Kennedy organization did

what it could to remedy this.

My problems with these nice old Republican ladies—who all looked alike, it seemed to me—began several days later when they started writing in for pictures and more pictures. Their letters became my curse in life. Invariably, they began: "Of course you remember me from _____, California, where I stood on the Senator's left that afternoon. I am sure a nice young man like you would not mind obliging a friend of the Kennedys by sending me six copies of . . ." Those letters still drift in several times a week. Some of these people even look me up when they visit New York.

Late in 1959 in California, there was a day that started terribly. We arrived in Oakland and were rushed to a meeting at a local hall. The Senator was supposed to speak at a luncheon, but somebody had been given the wrong date, so there was no luncheon. Instead, we went on to the next scheduled stop, Mills College. And, suddenly, a day of fiasco became a turning point! A small group of students clustered around the Senator and began asking questions. I noticed that for the first time Kennedy had started using his hands and talking persuasively. Politically he had been simmering, but he was starting to catch fire. And the girls, plus an occasional male graduate student, at Mills seemed to catch the sparks. They listened intently, threw probing and candid questions at him, and got replies that were just as candid and hard-hitting.

In California he also made good use of television. He never passed up a TV interview. And these effective local interviews, where he had to answer some tough questions and cope with the silly ones, proved good training for the Great Debates of 1960. He did as many radio interviews as he could, too. Sometimes, we'd arrive somewhere at midnight or later and there would be an invitation to appear on a local disk-jockey program. He was likely to drop in at the studio and talk to the platter-spinner and his listeners for as long as an hour.

Some of these people must have stayed up all through the night, because the attendance began to swell at his campaign breakfasts. They started drawing crowds of a thousand or more. And as the crowds increased, so did the Senator's animation. Even his handshakes had more vigor.

He often had been to early Mass before these precampaign breakfasts. Despite the stress of

Mrs. Kennedy with high-school students (left)
and with longshoreman (right) in Coos Bay, Oregon.

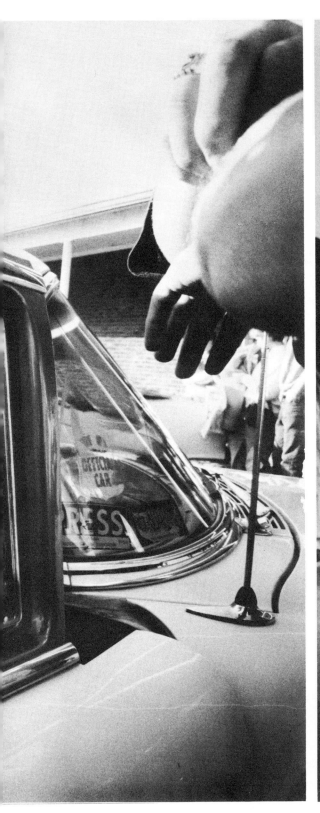

the campaign, he managed to maintain his religious obligations. With Jacqueline along, his health was in good hands, too.

My health suffered occasionally from the quick changes of scene, as we moved from sunny California to a blizzard in Wisconsin. We would fly in almost any weather; all Kennedy needed to go was word that his pilot, Howard Baer, thought we could make it. A seasoned commercial pilot, Baer had the tough job of deciding against pressure whether we could reach a certain spot by a given time. He often had to make a spot decision about whether he could fly the *Caroline* to the next town and make the return trip by motorcade. A slight, quiet, unruffled man, Baer kept his sense of humor through a grueling assignment. We bounced through storms and, while the rest of us said our prayers and searched for our stomachs, Kennedy would sit there calmly writing his speech and checking his schedule or even eating his chowder. He seemed quite unconcerned by the elements: he trusted Baer's flying ability. Even at an altitude of 10,000 feet, Kennedy seemed to have his feet on the ground. I began to consider him something of a fatalist.

On the second day of the year 1960, Kennedy held a news conference in the Senate Caucus Room in Washington. "I am announcing today my candidacy for the Presidency of the United States," he declared officially.

Reporters took notes and cameramen took pictures. Jacqueline Kennedy and some 300 friends and partisans applauded.

"For eighteen years," the Senator said, "I have been in the service of the United States, first as a naval officer in the Pacific during World War II and for the past fourteen years as a member of the Congress. In the last twenty years, I have traveled in nearly every continent and country—from Leningrad to Saigon, from Bucharest to Lima. From all of this, I have developed an image of America as fulfilling a noble and historic role as the defender of freedom in a time of maximum peril—of the American people as confident, courageous and persevering. It is with this image that I begin this campaign."

We were in a new phase of the preconvention campaign—the primaries. If you win them all, they can be excellent showcases. But they can also be fatal boobytraps.

In discussing the Kennedy family, I mentioned

the soul-searching that preceded the Senator's entry into the Wisconsin primary and the remarkable teamwork that ensued. Now we were here to test it.

Wisconsin started on a lonely level, a search for hands to shake and nonexistent votes to influence. Nobody seemed to care, few were willing to listen, no enthusiasm was apparent.

In a way, the Wisconsin primary was a tragedy too. It cast two great liberal Senators, with hardly any political differences between them, in the role of opponents. So there were few great issues discussed—but quite a few small ones. The Kennedy plane as against Hubert Humphrey's bus became an issue. Kennedy rightly pointed out that the plane was more efficient and actually cheaper—Humphrey said he "was a corner grocer running against a chain store." The bosses back east were an issue, and finally prejudice, Catholic against Protestant, became the issue—something Kennedy tried to avoid and Humphrey, a man well known for his liberalism, certainly abhorred.

Nevertheless, the campaign built and built and each morning it was like waking up and finding that a skyscraper was ten stories higher than it had been the night before. The crowds swelled, the enthusiasm grew, and the Senator's moral fiber became more apparent. I began to feel that the Democratic ship might not founder with someone other than Adlai Stevenson at the helm.

In March 1960, every fifth person in Wisconsin seemed to be a newsman or a polltaker. Of the other four, three were natives being interviewed by the out-of-towners. And the fifth man was either John F. Kennedy or his opponent, Hubert Humphrey. They got around the state so much that each candidate seemed like a thousand men.

Humphrey careened about Wisconsin in his bus. He dropped in at a bean feed and addressed a convention of well-diggers. One day, he talked himself speechless and a physician had to spray his throat back into action for a telecast.

Kennedy maintained the same frantic pace, but he tried to take a less folksy stand. The Kennedy women turned out in full force for his telethons. Viewers who phoned in questions gave them to one of the candidate's sisters or in-laws, who relayed them to Senator Kennedy.

As primary day neared, the reports from

grass-roots Wisconsin sounded good. And *The New York Times* noted that Kennedy was coming through as an "aggressive moderate," while Humphrey's image was that of a "strenuous liberal." An editor in Green Bay observed: "Somehow or other, Kennedy can advocate the same thing as Humphrey and still appear the more conservative of the two."

There were other, less learned comments from the Wisconsin forecasts:

A suburban matron in Brown Deer: "Kennedy's the picture of what I think we should have as President."

A doctor in Beaver Dam: "He has the dignity and polish compatible with the office."

A fundamentalist Baptist in La Crosse: "He's a nice big boy."

A housewife in Waukesha: "I wouldn't want Rome to take over in this country."

The Wisconsin voters posed some tough questions whenever they got a chance to meet the Senator from Massachusetts. One of the easiest, however, was asked by a registered nurse in Oconomowoc, who met Kennedy on his hand-shaking tour of the town's main street. As he grabbed this lady's hand, she asked him, "When did you have your last polio shot?"

"Oh, I had two shots about three years ago," Kennedy replied.

The woman took the would-be President by the arm and led him into a clinic. "Roll up your sleeve," she commanded.

Kennedy obeyed and was inoculated. When he offered to pay, the nurse lost some of her sternness. "It's on the house," she told the millionaire candidate.

The song of the day was "On, Wisconsin!" And on Tuesday, April 5, 1960, the state's Democrats (and quite a few Republicans who crossed over to participate in the fray) chose Kennedy by a 106,000-vote margin over Hubert Humphrey. Kennedy won 20½ of the state's 31 convention votes.

Unlike Wisconsin, the West Virginia primary seemed a pushover at the start. There appeared to be no problems and no opponents. But what seemed like a large victory in Wisconsin was in reality not decisive enough and Humphrey, who earlier had little hope of carrying even two districts in West Virginia, seemed encouraged by defeat in Wisconsin, and decided to enter the West Virginia primary.

Polls taken in late 1959 gave Kennedy a 70 to 30 per cent margin over Humphrey, but at this time, Humphrey hadn't been expected to enter the primary. A state with only a 3 per cent Catholic population, starving, high in unemployment, depending on government surpluses, it seemed difficult territory. Furthermore, the vote wasn't binding on the delegates. But in February, soon after Humphrey's registration, Kennedy also registered—only to find that instead of being the 70–30 certain victor, he was the 40–60 underdog; and the liberal Senator Humphrey awoke one day to find the conservative forces—and even the bigots—flocking to his camp.

Kennedy, who thought he had proved his strength in Wisconsin, had to prove it all over again. The Wisconsin victory meant nothing now.

He came into West Virginia prepared to tell the Democrats what he wanted to do about unemployment, care for the aged, distribution of surplus food, and relief for coal miners. But his religion became the chief issue. Historians may note that in the second half of the twentieth century he felt obliged to assure a West Virginia television audience: "If any Pope attempted to influence me as President, I would tell him it was completely improper."

On Sunday, April 10, a month before primary day, I took the overnight sleeper from New York to Parkersburg, West Virginia, where I had to report next day. In New York, while I had had a few days on my own, I photographed trapeze artists at the circus, as a kind of therapy. The parallel between a political campaign and a circus has often been cited, and as I traveled down the east coast to West Virginia, I couldn't help drawing the obvious comparisons. Of course, a campaign isn't all circus. It has its moments of serious purpose, high drama, and some of the tinsel and glitter of show business. The spectators also seem to have the same reactions. They want to be entertained, excited, and moved. The candidate's act is akin to the juggler's, as dangerous as the high-wire artist's, and sometimes resembles the marvelous clown's. This is said with no disrespect to any candidate. But what I love in the circus is what draws me to American politics, with all its uncertainty and suspense—you never know what will happen next.

It was with this sense of anticipation that I

arrived at Parkersburg, to find that the West Virginia campaign was already in full swing. At 7:45 on Monday morning, I tipped the porter at the bleak railroad station and made my way to the local Elks Hall, where Jack Kennedy had already made a speech. He was now mingling with the people, about two hundred in all, who had come for coffee and cookies. An organization called "West Virginians for Kennedy" had been set up months before and was now functioning efficiently.

The campaign issue, fanned by the nation's press, was now chiefly religion, in spite of the very real issues of grinding poverty, a high unemployment rate, and underindustrialization in West Virginia. Kennedy was still trying to stick to the main problems, and Humphrey, who certainly didn't want to be labeled a bigot or reactionary, avoided the religious question.

By now it had become clear that even if Humphrey won this primary, he would not get the nomination. He had really become the front man for the other candidates, who wanted to slow or stop the Kennedy drive.

Of course, Kennedy hammered this point home. "If Mr. Humphrey wins," he declared, "the chances of someone being nominated who doesn't understand the problems of West Virginia would be greatly enhanced. It seems to me it doesn't make any sense to vote for him when they [the stop-Kennedy forces] really favor someone else."

By this time Humphrey had acquired some strange political bedfellows. One of his supporters proved to be a Ku-Klux-Klansman, the conservative Harry Byrd organization backed him, and all sorts of reactionary and even lunatic-fringe groups were giving him support that only must have been a source of embarrassment to this great Senator.

Meanwhile, the Kennedy people, with their battle-tested Wisconsin troops led by Larry O'Brien, Kenny O'Donell, Robert Kennedy, *et al.,* were setting up an effective organization. The volunteers from Wisconsin, all high-caliber men, were now reinforced with an illustrious name—that of Franklin Delano Roosevelt, Jr. West Virginians still remembered his father as the man who had saved them in the early Thirties and who had helped them in their fight against the exploitation of that period. One opponent of Kennedy's to be reckoned with was John L. Lewis, president emeritus and spiritual head of the United Mine Workers.

This was the general situation in West Virginia at that time. But on the morning of my arrival I was mainly concerned with starting on the day's rounds. With a writer from the *Christian Science Monitor* I left the Elks Hall and joined a caravan headed for the next town. Our driver was a Kennedy volunteer. The *Monitor* man, who had come down to gather weighty material, asked the driver why he was for Kennedy. After a moment's hesitation, the West Virginian replied, "I don't rightly know, but I think it is his smile. That smile is worth a lot of votes—and don't think it's lost on the ladies either."

We received this intelligence with a heavy silence, while the weighty issues went out the window. The rest of the day wasn't much better. Most of the incidents I remember have aspects that brought me right back to the circus.

There was the moment when Kennedy, walking along the main street of the next town, which seemed totally deserted, approached a man at the corner with outstretched hand. "I am John Kennedy," he said. "I am running in the primary."

"Who?" asked the passer-by.

"John Kennedy. I am running in the Presidential primary."

"Oh!" And with a big burp the man let us know that he had already imbibed a couple of pints too many at that early hour of the morning.

Later, I raced along the highway in a state congressman's car, looking for Kennedy and a village called Ona. The old car kept stalling, and we drove back and forth frantically until we saw a commotion and realized we had passed Ona several times. We had missed the village because it had only one house facing the highway—and five more visible behind it.

Back at the hotel I found Jack de Nove, our television man, and his crew standing beside a maze of boxes and cables in the lobby. They were all in a high state of excitement. It seemed that their truck, containing all the day's films, had just burned down on the highway. Luckily, the driver was saved, but the crew was due in another state the following day, and their film was badly needed. While we discussed this tragicomedy, we saw Senator Humphrey, wearing his familiar Homburg, standing in another corner of the lobby and keeping his own counsel.

As the campaign went on, Kennedy was always on his toes, and we tried to keep up with him. After a late night shooting session with some miners, he asked me to send each of them a photograph. I took the foreman's name and he agreed to distribute the pictures. Weeks later, when we were about 2000 miles away, Kennedy asked, "Did you ever send those pictures to the miners, Jacques?" I was relieved to be able to answer yes—I had long since learned to appreciate his memory.

As the religious issue gained full force, Kennedy met it head-on. At a Baptist college a local minister rose and asked a leading question: Why had Kennedy refused to attend the blessing of an interdenominational chapel in Philadelphia? The question became a fifteen-minute statement of religious principles. Kennedy heard the man out patiently. Then he replied, point by point, calmly and logically. He hadn't attended the event because he was asked as an official representative of the Church. This he was not, and therefore he

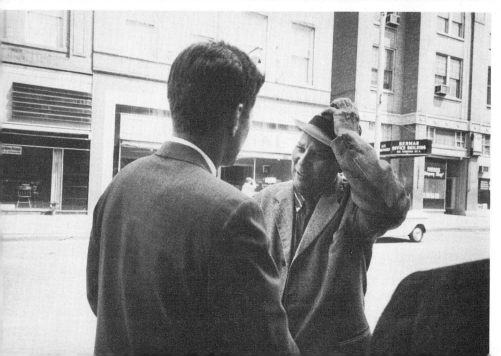

had declined. As a private citizen he would have gone. Then he discussed his convictions on his right to worship, his belief in separation of church and state, and gradually he grew more impassioned. Suddenly, before he could finish speaking, the whole audience rose and gave him a thunderous ovation. Certainly no one could call these people bigots.

Meanwhile, in his last-ditch efforts, Senator Humphrey was making a number of mistakes. He announced that he was going to appoint a Negro to the cabinet—and thus enraged the southern part of West Virginia. He accepted support from right-wing elements and angered the northern part of the state.

And he vainly tried to compete with the Kennedy clan. On a nationwide telecast he said, "My opponent, as you know, has lots of family. I have a family too. For example, here is my wife, Muriel." He pointed affectionately to the right, but his wife wasn't there. After several frantic shouts of "Muriel! where are you, Muriel?" his wife stood up in the back row of the hall. "Here I am, Hubert," she called out. "Come on up, Muriel, come on up," said the flustered Senator. "Show yourself to the folks."

On another occasion his twelve-year-old son was on a TV program. "What do you do, son?" the announcer asked. "I pass out pamphlets," young Humphrey replied. "And what happens?" asked the announcer. "Oh, I find a lot of people who won't take Dad's stuff," the boy answered.

On the Sunday before primary day, because of the opposition's tactics, Senator Kennedy issued the following statement: "In fourteen years of public life—in three campaigns for the House of Representatives and two for the United States Senate—I have never been subject to so much personal abuse." But he has never been a grudge-nurser. After the statement had been released, he was asked if he and Hubert Humphrey would ever be on friendly terms again. "I hope so," he replied; "but it may take a day or two."

Two days later, Tuesday, May 10, 1960, the citizens of West Virginia—on ballots that listed one hundred names in some counties—voted 212,000 for Kennedy and 136,000 for Humphrey. It had been a difficult battle, and in it prejudice as an issue had received a telling blow.

In a moving broadcast Senator Humphrey

withdrew from the Presidential race. "I am no longer a candidate for the Democratic Presidential nomination," he announced. Returning from Washington, where he had gone to wait out the uncertain returns, Senator Kennedy shook hands with his opponent and thanked the West Virginians. The same night he flew on to begin his campaign in Maryland.

But Wisconsin and West Virginia were the big struggles. Kennedy won the five other primaries he entered and was headed for the Democratic Convention at Los Angeles.

At this stage of the campaign, after a year of observing a political struggle from within, I had formed some strong impressions. First of all, I was now a fervent Kennedy-for-President man. My friends at the Village Independent Democrats, a Stevenson club in Greenwich Village, kept dropping by to look me over. What had happened to me? Had my own Catholicism swayed me? Had I gone mad?

I had started working for Kennedy with no political commitment and quite a few reservations. But since I had first known him I had found the Senator a decisive man of strong convictions. Listening to him daily, hearing him express so eloquently a political philosophy that I could believe in, convinced me that no one else could enter the White House so well qualified.

Another of my reactions—then and now—is that this democracy subjects a Presidential candidate to a terribly severe ordeal. He must crisscross the country many times; make thousands of speeches, shake thousands of hands; go without sleep; live out of a suitcase on planes, trains, and in hotel rooms—all this for more than

a year. And if his preliminary campaign goes well and he gets nominated by the convention, then he becomes eligible to begin this ritual all over again at a feverishly intensified pace.

After seeing the ordeal of the primary race I felt a great surge of pity for Adlai E. Stevenson, who had gone through it twice and had not been rewarded with the Presidency. John Kennedy had borne up well. I was sure he could survive a Presidential campaign, but I hoped he would have a few days of rest between primaries and the convention. Instead, there were meetings and more meetings.

Some of my professional encounters with the Senator shortly before the Democratic Convention may illustrate his state of mind. He was alternately jovial and fidgety.

Three days before leaving for the Democratic Convention, I flew to Hyannis Port to take color portraits and family pictures. Magazines and politicians were clamoring for them. When we got ready to shoot, Kennedy asked, "How do I look?"

"Fine—but I don't like your tie," I replied. "Here, why don't you wear mine?"

He glanced down and said, "Okay." We hastily exchanged ties, and after the picture was taken, he re-examined mine.

"That's a great tie!" he observed. "You must be making a lot of money these days."

"If I am," I told him, "it isn't from the Kennedy campaign."

But that tie later did make me some money. Somebody plagiarized my photo and it appeared on the cover of a European magazine. I received neither payment nor credit. It's ordinarily hard to prove theft of a photo, but my tie clinched my case. I was paid and credited.

In Hyannis Port, later that day we shot more pictures. Before we even started, he fidgeted and then asked me, "What do we need these pictures for? Are they necessary? If we don't take these pictures, is the world going to fall apart?"

"No, the world isn't going to fall apart," I replied. "But we might get a few more votes."

He grinned and said, "All right. Let's take the pictures."

I was shooting with a four-by-five camera, which meant that my subject had to sit pretty still. As I tried to focus, he kept jumping up, running to the telephone, and studying the latest issues of *Time* and *Newsweek,* each of which was carrying a story about him.

"What do you think of that cover on *Time*?" he asked.

"Senator," I said, "you really have to sit still, because I can't focus."

"All right. All right," he said. And he sat still for a few seconds. Then he picked up *Newsweek* and said, "Well, how do you like that cover? Don't you think it's better?"

"Yes, I think it is. But Senator, I can't focus unless you sit still."

He finally sat still—but as stiff as a statue. I managed four exposures before he said, "I think we have it now."

"No," I protested, "we don't have it at all."

"Oh, I think you've got it," he assured me.

"Okay," I said dubiously and a little dispiritedly. But as he walked out, he paused and asked, "Are you coming to the convention, Jacques?"

"You bet I am," I said.

"Good," he declared. "Let's take some great candids out there!"

*West Virginia miner listens
intently to Kennedy's speech to
midnight shift at coal mine.*

The convention

By jet plane one can fly from New York to Los Angeles in less than six hours. Getting through the lobby of the Biltmore Hotel during the Democratic Convention often took just as long. It was approximately as if someone had crammed a world's fair into one hotel in downtown Los Angeles.

Buttons, badges and posters, steel drums and orange juice—whatever the man who has everything didn't need—were being given away free. Lyndon B. Johnson's ladies distributed small orchids. The Kennedy people were giving out a PT-boat tieclasp. The Stevensonians were handing out texts of every speech Adlai had made since he had entered politics.

The Symingtonians struck me as the most inspired givers. They passed out fortune cookies with messages inside: America's fortunes lay in the hands of Stu Symington. They also had ball-point pens (that worked!) imprinted with this unbeatable ticket: SYMINGTON FOR PRESIDENT; KENNEDY FOR VICE-PRESIDENT; STEVENSON FOR SECRETARY OF STATE; NIXON FOR SPORTS WRITER. And, for delegates whose hands were unsteady when they shaved, the Symington people supplied adhesive strips bearing the legend STICK WITH SYMINGTON. One man, who wore six of them on his face, was either a loyal booster or an inept shaver.

I saw a dozen STOP KHRUSHCHEV buttons, but never found the time to buy one. Other vendors were peddling hats and sightseeing tours and hotel space, which certainly was scarce.

From Monday, July 11, through Wednesday, the day of the nominations, Kennedy visits an endless number of caucuses, questioning, answering, clarifying, disputing—an exhaustive and soul-searching process to win delegate support. Here are caucuses from Mississippi (upper left) *to Pennsylvania* (lower right).

But most people were selling candidates, and quite a few visitors were still shopping around.

The Lyndon Johnson-for-President crowd had platoons of Texas belles and lots of honkytonk hilarity. Even noisier were the supporters of Senator George Smathers, Florida's favorite son. They arrived with a big band and girls. Once Smathers reached town, they broadcast minute-by-minute bulletins of his progress into the city. A carpetbagger from Mars would have been sure that Smathers was a major contender, if not the front-runner.

At lobby level, Orval Faubus-for-President had his headquarters near the Kennedy reception center. Our headquarters was just as jolly and glad-handing as any of the others. The least hopeful section was Stuart Symington's, where this would-be compromise candidate was waiting patiently for a deadlocked convention. His only entertainment was provided by his son, a guitarist. Maybe the rest of his staff was busy distributing fortune cookies and adhesives. Later, Symington remarked—facetiously, I suppose—that if one more person congratulated him for having fought a clean campaign, he would punch him in the nose.

There were people in cowboy costumes who may have been cowboys and people in Eskimo costumes who probably were Eskimos. The Hawaiians were always in there pitching with their hulas. And as if the visiting firemen weren't sufficiently enlivening the local scene, the Los Angeles entrepreneurs decided to cash in, too. One day, an open car with about eight nearly naked girls passed outside the hotel and almost stampeded the crowd. They were, it turned out, sirens from a local night club that hoped to entice the big spenders. For a while, however, everybody thought they were campaigning for somebody.

Some local masseur was papering the delegates with cards asking, TIRED OF CAUCUSING? If so, his staff of international masseuses were operating twenty-four hours a day.

The famous and near-famous and obscure were all there in the Biltmore lobby. The House of Representatives parliamentarian could be seen taking orders from a cheeky bellhop. A governor was out pleading with a highway maintenance foreman for his wavering vote.

Upstairs, in Bob Kennedy's campaign headquarters, the activity was feverish but subdued.

Mostly, men in shirtsleeves were checking lists of names, sifting reports of defections in the Kennedy camp, and following up rumors of splits in the enemy camps.

The enemy, in turn, was spreading rumors of defections in Kennedy's home state. In the Biltmore lobby, a man was seen brandishing a MASSACHUSETTS FOR JOHNSON placard. Asked where he was from, he replied, "Suh, ah'm from Lubbock!" After that, the brass band from Texas, Johnson's state, was trailed by an enormous fat man waving a sign, TEXAS IS BIG FOR KENNEDY.

There were fifteen or twenty Kennedy listening posts, conference rooms, and press rooms in the hotel. Newsmen were everywhere, living four to a room and even sharing typewriters. Since this was the week end before the convention opened, they were mostly interviewing each other.

Not everybody could be accommodated at the Biltmore, and many key figures didn't even know where they would be staying until they arrived at the Los Angeles airport. Whole delegations were often dispatched to motels many miles away from the center of activity. Invariably, these delegations were paired on the philosophy that opposites attract. One California motel housed a Deep South delegation and a Far West contingent. These particular Southerners were hard-drinking hedonists who closed most evenings by staggering into the motel's swimming pool. Nearly every one of them seemed to be either a judge or a colonel. The Westerners were sturdy, severe-looking people with Gary Cooper faces and an "early-to-bed, early-to-rise" way of life. They rarely touched anything harder than

From left: Hy Raskin with visitor at Kennedy headquarters; Robert Kennedy with Neal Staebler and Averell Harriman at Los Angeles. Below: Brothers Teddy and Robert, brother-in-law Steve Smith (standing), in private conference.

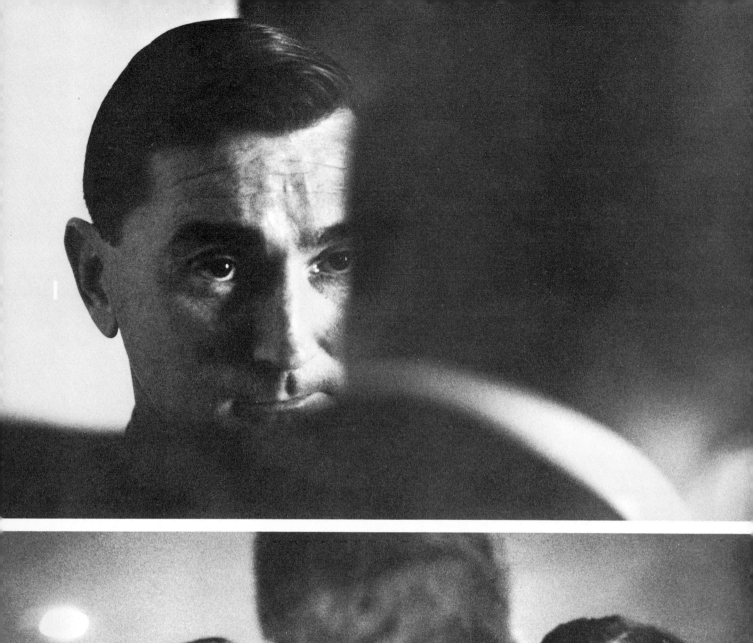

Coca-Cola and they pulled their curtains tight whenever the Southerners acted up, which was most of the time. But part of a convention's appeal is its ludricious combinations of people, manners, and customs.

The candidates began arriving, with varying degrees of pomp and ceremony. Adlai Stevenson came to town last—with a big parade and not just one band, but seven; not just a hundred demonstrators, but a thousand. It was staged by professionals with all the zest of a Metro-Goldwyn-Mayer finale.

Kennedy's arrival was less flamboyant, but more triumphant. There were five or six hundred people at the airport, where a Virgin Islands steel band played, Kennedy volunteer girls snake-danced around the terminal, and Hawaiians decorated the Senator with a lei. There was also one fight—between the driver of a KENNEDY FOR PRESIDENT truck and a saboteur who tried to paste a Stevenson sticker on it.

Senator Kennedy was confident. He had learned that Terry Sanford, the Democratic nominee for governor of North Carolina, was bringing at least a third of his delegation into the Kennedy camp. This was an inroad into the Solid South. And Kennedy told reporters who met his plane: "I think, without counting any support from Pennsylvania, California, New Jersey, Iowa, Kansas, and Minnesota, I will have over 600 votes on the first ballot." He needed 761 to win.

He was asked to comment on Lyndon Johnson's contention that Kennedy was short on experience. "I expect to defeat Senator Johnson by the end of the week," he observed, "and I wonder what that will do to him." (As it turned out, the defeat did Johnson a lot of good.) As Kennedy drove toward the Biltmore, the crowds grew thicker and thicker. People were waving and shouting. This was obviously the heavyweight candidate arriving, coming to town to win his championship.

JFK with Kenneth O'Donnell (above) *and Robert and Steve Smith* (below).

Once he had checked in at his suite on the fourteenth floor, he seldom left. For me it was an ideal photographic situation. For the next six days I was practically locked in with the leading contender.

Kennedy's suite started out with three rooms—a reception room; a living room, which became a waiting room; and a bedroom, where he held his conferences. Each day, however, he had to add an extra room to cope with the increasing volume of business callers.

Occasionally he slipped out to visit one of the state delegations. The big feat was to get into the elevator with him, for it held about eight or nine people. Once you missed it you might as well give up, for after JFK arrived in the lobby, the crowd swallowed him up. He would appear in the last room of his suite and dash for the elevator. As soon as the press, standing about fifty feet away, spotted him, an incredible stampede of rolling TV cameras, lights, reporters, photographers, and microphones would roar after him. I consider the fact that I never missed the elevator one of my major achievements at the convention. But then I did have a head start of something like fifty feet.

At the convention, his family was functioning like the Strategic Air Command. Working out of the Senator's suite was his brother-in-law Steve Smith, who either accompanied the Senator when he left or stayed behind to receive and transmit urgent messages via mobile phone. Another brother-in-law, Sargent Shriver, was handling interracial, big-business, farm, and labor relations. He was the emissary and was in and out of the suite several times a day. (Jacqueline Kennedy, who was pregnant, did not come to the convention.)

Robert Kennedy worked on the lower floor in the famous Suite 8315, in which he met with delegation leaders and tried to keep his finger on the pulse of the convention. Working with him were his brother Teddy and ex-football player Byron "Whizzer" White, now Bobby's deputy in the Justice Department. Larry O'Brien, now the President's special assistant for Congressional relations, had a similar assignment in Los Angeles. Larry had a file on every delegate. He knew where each delegate was, what he was doing, and what he was dreaming about. I consider Larry a political genius. I remember hearing him rebuke an aide who had just wandered in from a hard day of buttonholing: "You mean you've been gone a whole day and all you've got me is one-half vote?" But even the slightest gain was meaningful. Kenny O'Donnell, working mostly outside, completed the team that had been so well tested in the primaries. Ted Sorensen, another key adviser, was handling the egghead department. He and his group went to the caucuses and presented Kennedy's ideas.

Behind the ground-floor reception room, Hy Raskin—a handsome, stocky, red-faced lawyer with silvery hair—ran a special room for delegates. Raskin had twice worked for Stevenson's election and ended up deputy national chairman. His experience with older delegates was invaluable at the convention, and later on in the Western States.

On the fourth floor, Pierre Salinger, an old friend of mine, made life easier for newsmen who poured into Kennedy's press headquarters. Here, among coffee machines and cigar smoke the amiable Pierre was getting his first workout with the national press. Among the inner guard of Kennedy advisers, Pierre took a somewhat special place. Neither Boston Irish nor old-line politician, he was a former city editor of the San Francisco *Chronicle,* a *Collier's* editor, and an investigator for the McClellan committee before he joined the Kennedy staff. Half-Jewish, half-Catholic, and all Democrat, he naturally

thrived on the confusion and chaos that surrounds a national election.

I had first worked with Pierre as part of a writer-photographer team for the now-defunct *Collier's* during the Hungarian uprising. We did an article on a Hungarian refugee family that had been involved in the revolt and had tragic experiences to relate. We were both close to tears; Pierre identified completely with this family—and then wrote one of the most moving stories to come out of that period. Even today, five years later, when he gets anywhere near McKeesport, Pa., where the family was resettled, he calls them to check on their welfare.

He has a colossal love of life—he likes good food and wine, is a fine pianist, smokes enormous cigars of Winston Churchill size, he loves parties and people, and his sense of humor and fund of stories are inexhaustible. His exposé of the Teamsters Union, on which he spent six months of research, brought him to the attention of Robert Kennedy. Eventually he became a major investigator for Bobby. In September 1959 Pierre joined the Kennedy campaign staff.

Early in the convention, Lyndon Johnson and Adlai Stevenson began to show disturbing signs of strength. Johnson made a few civil-rights statements that won him a border-state delegate here and there. The Stevenson flutter was threatening to become an explosion, even though the

excitement wasn't so much among delegates as it was in the news stories. Symington kept losing strength. When he got there he was a candidate; by the day the convention opened he was virtually a tourist.

One of the most frightening aspects of the convention was the fickleness of delegates. Idealism sometimes went out the door—sometimes for political gain or personal power, sometimes just out of restlessness. Many times Senator Kennedy visited a caucus where he could have compromised. But he stuck to his guns, and never did I see him dilute his political philosophy. He was equally fearless and uncompromising in closed meetings with big business or labor leaders. When these people tried to adulterate his pronouncements or make him restate them a trifle less sharply, he told them: "Gentlemen, I have made my statement. That's what I believe. That's what I'm going to do." And he went to the balloting indebted to no one.

One of the Southern delegations asked him if he believed the Supreme Court's rulings on integration were moral. The Senator said yes, and added that he was one hundred per cent in favor of the Court's action. He also answered a labor question put by a Michigan delegate, where labor is powerful, in a manner that left no doubt about his independence of any pressure groups.

At a Democratic National Committee dinner he quoted Longfellow to his audience:

Lawrence (Larry) O'Brien, oldest (forty-three) of the immediate campaign staff.

Sargent Shriver (left) *with Chuck Roche. Robert Kennedy with David McDonald of the Steelworkers. Pierre Salinger* (right).

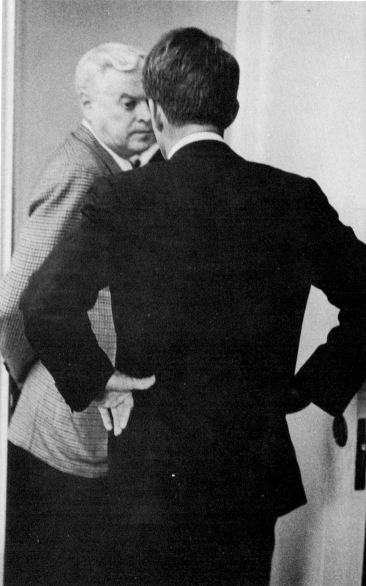

"...Humanity with all its fears,
With all its hopes of future years,
Is hanging breathless on thy fate."

And at a National Association for the Advancement of Colored People rally, he quoted Sir Francis Bacon: "There is hope enough and to spare—not only to make a bold man try but also to make a sober-minded man believe." To which he added with assurance: "I am bold enough to try."

At the Pennsylvania caucus breakfast, Kennedy and Symington and Johnson appeared jointly. Johnson made a resounding campaign speech. Symington made a speech that sounded to me like a gentlemanly funeral oration for himself. Kennedy simply stated his principles and left. He didn't wait around for bargaining.

When the candidates' paths crossed, they would indulge in a minimum of banter and then work on their speeches or bury their heads in their hands for a moment of rest. But they were always cordial. In American politics, it seems, even mortal enemies behave like good friends in each other's presence—if nowhere else.

The last tense caucus was Texas. Lyndon Johnson made a ringing denunciation of Kennedy to his home team. Although he had always spoken highly of the Senator from Massachusetts, the Senate majority leader now bitterly accused him of absenteeism. Jack and Bobby Kennedy sat behind Johnson and listened tensely to this oration. Then Kennedy stood up, outlined his philosophy, ignored Johnson's accusations, and successfully eliminated Johnson at his own caucus.

On Wednesday, July 13, 1960, the day of nominating and balloting, the Senator moved from the Biltmore to the seclusion of an eight-room apartment. This setting was as improbable as the rest of California. The apartment house was built like a ship. Kennedy's suite, in which he watched the convention on television, was called the "top deck." The place where the newsmen hovered anxiously was several stories below, and was referred to as "cabin class."

I abandoned the Senator temporarily and paid my first visit to the Los Angeles Memorial Sports Arena, where the convention was being held. Before going on the convention floor, I checked in at a house the Kennedys had rented just outside. It was part of a forthcoming housing show at the Sports Arena. The Johnson

Lyndon Johnson, in his last effort to wrest the nomination away from JFK, invited him to the Texas caucus, where he accused Kennedy of absenteeism in the Senate. Kennedy ignored the charges. This was the last round before the balloting began.

118

forces had also taken one of the cottages. The Symington staff had a trailer. The Kennedy "model house" was an elaborate set-up with direct telephone lines to several delegations and to all the Kennedy workers on the floor. There were also walkie-talkies, controlled by Hy Raskin.

The huge Arena was air-conditioned. Many of the old-timers said it was a considerable improvement over the good old sweaty days in the Chicago stockyards, but the 15,000 people jammed into the Sports Arena seemed to be sweating plenty. When I arrived, long speeches were placing the candidates in nomination. I was impressed by the exuberance and good will that marked the demonstrations after each nomination. In that steamy convention hall, they were excellent ways of letting off steam regardless of loyalties. Quite a few of those fervent Symington demonstrators seen on television were Kennedy people, just helping out a fellow Democrat in distress. I saw a woman who had been an outspoken Kennedy supporter since early 1959 swinging a Symington sign with great vigor. I was sure she hadn't defected. The show had to go on!

Of all the candidates the one least seen but most discussed was Adlai Stevenson, who practically broke my heart in Los Angeles. This man seemed to want, at the same moment, to be and not to be President. But his failure to support Kennedy was proving divisive. Did he want Lyndon Johnson to win the nomination? Certainly not, I was sure. Yet his exquisite hesitation almost brought about that result. Kennedy was also visibly disappointed. He had placed Stevenson's name in nomination in 1956. Up to the last possible moment, he hoped that Stevenson would now return the favor. Instead, that honor went to Governor Orville Freeman of Minnesota. Kennedy was the man who could "bring courage and drive and dedication at a time when it is desperately called for in America and the world," Governor Freeman told the assembly.

The Minnesota delegation was the most schizophrenic body at the convention. Governor Freeman was for Kennedy; Hubert Humphrey was for Stevenson. (When Kennedy had addressed the Minnesota caucus, Humphrey had introduced him as an "old friend.") Several diehard delegates were still for Humphrey. Minnesota's junior Senator, Eugene McCarthy, declared for Johnson—then made a last-minute switch and ended up delivering Adlai Stevenson's nominat-

ing speech. McCarthy's address turned out to be the oratorical highlight of the convention. It was close to demagoguery.

"Do not turn away from this man," McCarthy pleaded. "Do not reject this man. He has fought gallantly. He has fought courageously. He has fought honorably. In 1952 in the great battle. In 1956 he fought bravely. And between those years and since he has stood off the guerrilla attacks of his enemies and the sniping attacks of those who should have been his friends. Do not reject this man who made us all proud to be called Democrats. Do not reject this man who, his enemies said, spoke above the heads of the people, but they said it only because they didn't want the people to listen. He spoke to the people. He moved their minds and stirred their hearts. This was what was objected to. Do not leave this prophet without honor in his own party. Do not reject this man."

Roars and arm-flinging answered his pleas. I have known Gene McCarthy for years. He is a mild-mannered former professor, steeped in Catholic theology, but I had difficulty recognizing him that day. His target seemed to be Kennedy, a fellow Catholic and, like himself, a liberal.

The frantic demonstration that followed Stevenson's nomination was bewildering. It had none of the good-natured camaraderie that char-

acterized all the other outpourings of loyalty. The other demonstrations had been Americana of sorts. This was a fanatical, hysterical rite of a kind I had never seen. Hundreds of wild-eyed rioters, bobbing and weaving, chanting and shrieking, seethed up and down the aisles. They had a huge papier-mâché snowball which they kept aloft like a volleyball. Men and women wearing Mother Hubbards labeled STEVENSON, snake-danced along the balcony steps. The entire gallery had become a veritable sea of Stevenson posters, swinging wildly back and forth.

There were kids with beards and guitars and banners. Some wore turtleneck sweaters; many were too young to vote. Each had a whistle or a harmonica or some other noisemaker. There was also a twenty-piece band. Delegates covered their ears in a vain effort to keep the volume at a dull roar.

I stood in the center of this storm and I was frightened. The chant of *"We want Stevenson! We want Stevenson! We want Stevenson!"* had an effect like voodoo on the chanters. It was almost a religious expression of rebellion—not against Democrats or Republicans, but seemingly against the whole world they lived in.

A well-known actress and three other girls were dancing near where I stood. They whirled around to the drumlike *"We want Stevenson!"*

And they couldn't seem to stop. Gene McCarthy was pleading with all these people to calm down, but none of them could—even if they had wanted. They seemed completely out of control. It was a spectacle I prefer not to see again at a political event.

The demonstration had been carefully staged by professional Stevensonians and Hollywood was represented by such ardent Stevensonians as Vincent Price, Clifford Odets, Lee Remick, and Henry Fonda. While each candidate had been issued passes for 125 demonstrators, the Stevenson "professionals" had hit upon passing the passes back as they entered. It is unknown how many actually got in, but the number was estimated at 500 to 600.

Many people in that hall were appalled by what they saw. Governor Leroy Collins of Florida, the chairman, was clearly shocked when he told the rioters to keep it up "if you want the name of this convention associated with hoodlumism."

The demonstration scarcely had the desired effect. Even if delegates are fickle, they are essentially decent citizens who want their country governed by the best possible man. Somehow they know that no matter how they vote, their country is not going to be ruined by the man they select. And when they witnessed this outburst of fanaticism, some of them said, "If that's Stevenson, I don't want any part of him."

It wasn't Stevenson. It bore no resemblance to the urbane, civilized statesman these hysterical people were acclaiming. But if this is what one man's hesitation can produce, then I thank my lucky stars that John F. Kennedy is a decisive man. After twenty-five minutes, with persistent gaveling by Governor Collins, and a two-minute period when all lights were turned off it finally subsided.

There were many dark horses and favorite sons to be nominated and seconded before the balloting began. Such formidable contenders as Governors Docking of Kansas and Loveless of Iowa were placed effusively in nomination, only to be withdrawn before the balloting opened. Last and least of the nominees was Governor Ross Barnett of Mississippi, a white-supremacist whose nominator declared: "Through his veins flows the finest blood that has been produced in America."

The balloting began. I stood with Larry O'Brien, who held a list of Kennedy's estimated strength in each delegation. Larry had his figures with him. We would win with 762 votes—one more than the necessary majority—on the first

124

Convention delegates listen to balloting in moods ranging from intense and uncertain to skeptical and fatigued.

ballot. That was his conservative estimate. But as the votes were announced, he began adding and subtracting. I was too tense to watch his computations.

During the balloting, there was a churchlike feeling in the hall. This was both the business of the convention and the nation's destiny in the making.

I stood there, nearly frozen despite the heat. Occasionally, coming back from an almost unreal world, I would ask, "How are we doing, Larry?"

"We're going to make it. We're going to make it," he assured me—and himself.

Late in the first ballot, Wyoming put us over the top. Bobby Kennedy knew that ten of Wyoming's fifteen votes were for his brother Jack. At that point, Kennedy had 750 votes. Dodging like a halfback along the crowded floor, Bobby closed in on the Wyoming chairman, Tracy S. McCracken. "Ten won't do it, but eleven will!" Bobby cried. McCracken threw up his hands and said, "Let 'em all go!" Thus Wyoming gained the glory of nominating the winner.

Everyone started shouting and screaming, but it took me a few minutes to realize that we were in. I didn't really grasp it until I saw Patricia Kennedy jumping up and down like a girl on a diving board. A dozen people were pumping her hand or kissing her. She tossed her hat in the air. Teddy Kennedy grabbed the Wyoming standard and waved it high.

It took a while for the noise to subside, the final votes to be cast, and the final vote changes

to be recorded. The official first ballot totals were:

Senator John F. Kennedy of Massachusetts	806
Senator Lyndon B. Johnson of Texas	409
Senator Stuart Symington of Missouri	86
Adlai E. Stevenson	79½
Governor Robert Meyner of New Jersey	43
Senator Hubert Humphrey of Minnesota	41½
Senator George Smathers of Florida	30
Governor Ross Barnett of Mississippi	23
Governor Herschel Loveless of Iowa	1½
Governors Pat Brown of California, Orval Faubus of Arkansas, and Albert Rosellini of Washington	½ vote each

A few minutes later the vote was made unanimous, and then we waited for the chosen man to appear. It took a long time, and there was no room in which to move. But my cameras and I were in a good position atop a chair, where I stayed for hours. Finally Kennedy arrived. In the hall were most of the Kennedys who had worked so hard for this moment. Mrs. Rose Kennedy, the Robert Kennedys and four of their children, the Ted Kennedys, the Shrivers and one son, the Steve Smiths, and the Lawfords and three children. John Kennedy appeared on the dais with his mother and sister Pat, and the others went up to greet him.

It was early Thursday morning when JFK made his brief speech from the platform. "This is in many ways the most important election in the history of our country," he told the convention. "All of us are united in our devotion to this country. We wish to keep it strong and free. It requires the best of all of us. I can assure all of you here who have reposed this confidence in me that I'll be worthy of your trust."

It wasn't a classic speech, but people were weeping. A man waved a 1932 newspaper with accounts of Franklin Delano Roosevelt's nomination. A woman was shouting, but she was so

hoarse that she wasn't making a sound. All the state standards were thrust forward together. And the Democratic party had a candidate for President.

That night, in the Kennedy house across from the convention hall, there was a small celebration, but it was a hushed affair. Here was the new standard-bearer of the Democratic Party, and all had come to pay homage. His family and staff were there. And so were the nation's political leaders—among them Governor Lawrence of Pennsylvania; Harriman, De Sapio, Wagner from New York; Ribicoff and Bayley from Connecticut; Mike di Salle from Ohio; Mayor Daley of Chicago; G. Mennen Williams of Michigan; and many others. But what impressed me most was the hush, the almost silent recognition of a new leader. I had thought this moment would be full of laughter, jovial post-morteming, and anecdotes.

In the morning I reported to the candidate's hotel suite at eight o'clock. He and Bobby had been pondering the choice of a Vice-Presidential nominee when Lyndon Johnson had come through with a particularly warm telegram of congratulations. Johnson had also been quoted as wisecracking that L.B.J. now stood for "Let's Back Jack." Perhaps the Texan's harsh words were now forgotten.

Shortly after I had arrived and congratulated him, the nominee phoned Johnson. His wife, Lady Bird, answered. Her husband was sleeping, but she awoke him. Lyndon Johnson agreed to meet Kennedy two hours later in the Johnson suite.

At 10:15 a.m. the two former adversaries were together. I shot a photo of them conferring, with Kennedy looking pensive and Johnson sipping a soft drink. Kennedy asked Johnson if he was available for the Vice-Presidency, and the Texan said he was. Each then went off to discuss the match with his own advisers.

During the day, Kennedy met with Governor David Lawrence of Pennsylvania, Governor Abraham Ribicoff of Connecticut, Mike di Salle of Ohio, Adlai Stevenson, Walter Reuther, and other Democratic well-wishers. Virtually all the previous night's nominees had been considered as running mates. So had Senators Engle of California and Jackson of Washington, as well as Governors Freeman of Minnesota and Nelson of Wisconsin.

Early Thursday morning Kennedy accepts the nomination. "I can assure all of you here . . . that I will be worthy of your trust." Some people were weeping.

131

Left : *In Kennedy's headquarters the morning after nomination, hopeful candidates and advisors consult on crucial selection of Vice Presidential candidate. Below : Kennedy meets with Senator Lyndon Johnson, his final choice.*

By four-thirty in the afternoon, Kennedy was convinced that Lyndon B. Johnson would be the strongest possible running mate. He phoned the Texan again to see if he'd changed his mind.

"Jack, if you want me to run, I'll do it," said Johnson.

Bobby Kennedy warned Johnson that there might be a fight on the convention floor, but Johnson was determined. "If Jack wants me for Vice-President, I'm willing to make a fight for it," he told Bobby. Then Kennedy made the announcement.

It was greeted with some dismay, but I think Kennedy's choice of Lyndon Johnson typifies his pragmatic liberalism. He needed the votes of the South to win the election. And as President he could not function efficiently with the conservative Johnson running the Senate. By neutralizing him in the Vice-Presidency, Kennedy had everything to gain and little to lose. It proved to be one of Kennedy's shrewdest moves.

G. Mennen Williams angrily called it a "mistake" and one Americans for Democratic Action official called it a "double cross"—but once the shock had passed, the maneuver was hailed as a master stroke. Johnson won easily. And the Democratic Party knew who was its boss!

Kennedy was in great physical shape when he was nominated. During the campaign—when he seldom had time to eat or sleep—he *gained* weight. He has a remarkable constitution.

On Friday the convention switched to the Los Angeles Coliseum, where the Dodgers customarily caucus. The Coliseum's seating capacity of 100,000 was ideal for the Democratic show of unity—some called it the "love feast," others the "pagan ritual." We rode in a triumphant motorcade from the Biltmore to the Coliseum.

All the players were there to take their bows at this grand finale—Humphrey, Symington, Speaker of the House Sam Rayburn, Mrs. Eleanor Roosevelt, Stevenson, everybody. Henry Jackson, the incoming party chairman, and Paul Butler, the outgoing chairman, were there, of course. Everyone had a chance to speak, so the celebration, which began in broad daylight, lasted late into the night. And it was there that John Fitzgerald Kennedy proclaimed the New Frontier.

"The New Frontier is here, whether we seek it or not," he declared. "Beyond that frontier are uncharted areas of science and space, unsolved

Two brothers make the final decision.

problems of peace and war, unconquered pockets of ignorance and prejudice, unanswered questions of poverty and surplus."

"It would be easier to shrink from that New Frontier, to look to the safe mediocrity of the past, to be lulled by good intentions and high rhetoric—and those who prefer that course should not vote for me or the Democratic Party."

"But I believe that the times require imagination and courage and perseverance. I'm asking each of you to be pioneers toward the New Frontier. My call is to the young in heart, regardless of age—to the stout in spirit, regardless of party—to all who respond to the scriptural call, 'Be strong and of courage; be not afraid, neither be dismayed.'"

Senator Kennedy was addressing the nation—but he could have been talking directly to all his campaign workers—when he said: "It has been a long road . . . to this crowded convention city. Now begins another long journey, taking me into your cities and homes across the United States. Give me your help, and your hand, and your voice."

The Coliseum shook with the crowd's roar.

On Saturday the new Democratic Party had its first full-dress meeting. How were *we* (for me, it was now *we,* not *they*) going to approach the campaign? How were we going to raise money? Even after I had become familiar with the high costs of campaigning, I could never adjust to hearing a Kennedy discussing shortages of funds.

On Sunday, July 17, 1960, we flew from Los Angeles to Boston on the *Kennedy Special,* an American Airlines jet. It was an exhilarating flight. Senator Kennedy played with his brother Bobby's children. Some of us just slept until a noisy crowd—15,000 people, 400 policemen, and four bands—awakened us in Boston.

The plane had made the cross-country trip in four hours and fifty-eight minutes, slightly ahead of schedule. Although this was an auspicious start for the Presidential campaign, its pace was to quicken in the months to come.

Kennedy announces the Johnson choice to the press.

*The party, united
again under the
standard bearer, at
the acceptance
ceremonies at
the Los Angeles
Coliseum.*

The first meeting of the new party, under the chairmanship of Henry M. Jackson, took place in the Senator's suite. Most of his close advisers are present. The issues under discussion were finances (there was no money), organization, and personnel.

The
campaign

"Weren't there enough news cameramen in the campaign?" I have been asked frequently.

The answer is "Yes, and some of the best, too."

It is not too difficult to explain that there is a use for a photo-journalist in modern campaigning. I had three principal missions. One was to supply photos of Senator Kennedy for Democratic brochures. The photos, like the texts, were slanted toward specialized viewpoints—JFK and the aged, JFK and minority problems, JFK and labor, JFK and the businessman. Many were in foreign languages; others were of the "Facts for New Voters" and "John F. Kennedy: Man for the '60s" varieties.

Then there were giveaway photos. Many small dailies and rural weeklies don't have photographers of their own. I was able to furnish them on-the-spot photo coverage, for which they were grateful even though the majority of their editors came out for the Republican candidate, Vice-President Richard M. Nixon. And thousands of my pictures of Kennedy were farmed out to state chairmen and party organizations, which gave them away or sold them to raise funds.

And then there were campaign buttons. The photos on most official Kennedy-for-President buttons were my handiwork. So were letterheads and hatbands. We also put out a New Frontier tabloid newspaper at regular intervals. There were stickers; my favorites read J'AIME JACK and VIVA KENNEDY. There were also advertisements and posters.

I would travel with Kennedy for two weeks at a time. Then I would rush back to New

144

*Senator Kennedy aloft in the Caroline studies
campaign tactics with group of advisors.*

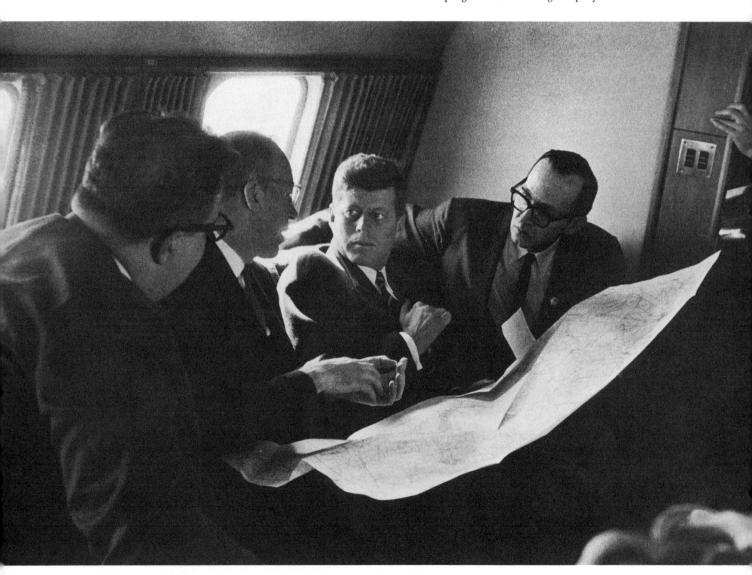

*The candidate
in rare moment
of solitary reflection
en route to California.*

York, process my photos, and turn them over to the Democratic National Committee for distribution.

In addition, my regular magazine clients were clamoring for photo spreads. I could scarcely keep up with the demand. After he became President, John F. Kennedy jested that I was the only person who made money on the New Frontier. This is not quite the case, I am not one to contradict the President of the United States.

As a matter of fact, I am short five dollars. Like most rich men, Kennedy seldom travels with much cash on hand. Somewhere along the line, his credit wasn't good and he had to borrow from his photographer. And he's the only President who owes me money.

The badges for the official campaign party were signed by party chairman Henry Jackson. On the badges, at least, his signature was of John Hancock proportions. In Peoria, Illinois, a burly local photographer tried to ride in our car, but there was no room. We had to ease him out. He swore to avenge this slight and, as proof of his intentions, he looked at the badge of an authorized photographer. "Okay," he growled. "I'll remember your name, Henry M. Jackson. I'll get you, Henry M. Jackson, if it's the last thing I ever do in Peoria!"

Half an hour later, at the City Hall, I was struck a tremendous blow from behind. The Peoria Avenger had decided that *I* was the evil Henry Jackson. We scuffled in the middle of a huge crowd, which was interested only in Senator Kennedy and not in the preliminary events. Using a brand-new camera lens as a weapon, I managed to stun my assailant with a blow on the head. But it cost me sixty-five dollars' worth of equipment.

There were, however, very few such mishaps during the campaign. As the campaign went on, organization became superb. At worst, a bag got lost. And once I walked into a hotel room to find a woman sleeping in my bed. There had been a minor error in assigning rooms.

But the advance men's errors were negligible and their reliability astonishing. Their timing had to be precise, as this agenda (with my interpolated comments) for one day of the Kennedy campaign—a Saturday spent in Missouri and Kansas—would indicate:

3:00 a.m. (C.D.T.)   Arrive Lambert Airport, St. Louis. Motorcade to Park Plaza Motel.

(We arrived two hours late, which simply meant two hours' less sleep.)

9:15 a.m.   Democratic Breakfast, Park Plaza Motel.

9:30 a.m.   Depart Park Plaza Motel by motorcade.

(Before departing, Kennedy made an unscheduled speech to the crowd waiting outside the motel.)

9:35 a.m.   Arrive Crestwood Shopping Center and Rally

10:05 a.m.   Depart Crestwood Shopping Center.

10:50 a.m.   Arrive Northland Shopping Center. Rally.

11:20 a.m.   Depart Northland Shopping Center.

11:30 a.m.   Arrive Lambert Airport

12 Noon   Depart Lambert Airport for Joplin, Mo.

12:20 p.m. (C.S.T.)   Arrive Joplin. Airport rally.

(We shifted time zones several times a day. We were constantly leaving one place at three o'clock and arriving at the next at two-thirty.)

1:05 p.m.   Depart Joplin for Wichita, Kansas.

2:15 p.m.   Arrive Wichita Airport. Motorcade to Lawrence Stadium.

2:30 p.m.   Arrive Lawrence Stadium.

3:00 p.m.   Depart Lawrence Stadium for Wichita Airport.

3:30 p.m.   Leave Wichita Airport.

4:30 p.m.   Arrive Richards-Gebaur Air Force Base, Grandview. Motorcade to Truman Shopping Center.

4:45 p.m.   Arrive Truman Shopping Center, Grandview. Rally.

5:15 p.m.   Depart Truman Shopping Center.

5:45 p.m.   Arrive Muehlebach Hotel, Kansas City, Mo. Rest and dinner alone (for Senator Kennedy).

147

*As the campaign mounted, a feverish
feeling began to grip both the candidate
and the crowds. First the women and
slowly the men also began responding
to JFK in larger and wilder
demonstrations until finally, toward
the end of the campaign, it became
almost impossible for the candidate to
make an uninterrupted speech or even
talk about his program.*

Charleston, West Virginia.

Next page: *Political meeting in California.*
The smoke-filled room is air-conditioned now.

(This event alone made that day a lighter one than most. On an average day, we would hit some twenty different places.)

8:00 p.m.	Depart hotel for Auditorium.
8:30 p.m.	Television speech from Auditorium.
9:15 p.m.	Depart Auditorium by motorcade for Kansas City, Kansas.
9:30 p.m.	Arrive Fund-Raising Dinner at Shawnee Mission East High School, Kansas City, Kansas.
9:45 p.m.	Depart Fund-Raising Dinner at Shawnee Mission East High School, Kansas City, Kansas.
10:00 p.m.	Arrive Richards-Gebaur Air Force Base.
10:15 p.m.	Depart for Green Bay, Wisconsin.
12:45 a.m. Sunday	Arrive Green Bay.

(We arrived ninety minutes late.)

This particular agenda required six advance men. In addition to making all the arrangements listed above, they had set up a working press room with full transmitting facilities at the Park Plaza Motel; lined up telephones and Western Union runners at the Crestwood and Northland Shopping Centers and at Joplin Airport; arranged for interphone service in the press section and telegraph facilities at Lawrence Stadium, Truman Shopping Center, and Shawnee Mission East High School, and reserved press rooms with complete facilities at the Muehlebach and the Auditorium.

Advance men thought of everything, as these excerpts from an agenda will indicate:

STAFF ROOMS: Located on 14th floor. Staff preregistered. Room assignments listed alphabetically. Keys to rooms assigned to staff members are in the doors.

STAFF AND PRESS BAGGAGE: Delivered to the receiving entrance and taken via the service elevators to the rooms in which the guests are registered.

TELEPHONE SWITCHBOARD: The switchboard is handled by five operators and one supervisor. Hotel Statler Hilton has a direct dialing system, permitting guests to dial either local or long-distance calls.

ELEVATORS: Six passenger and four service elevators with operators. Two passenger elevators will be set aside for the use of Senator Kennedy and his Official Party at all times.

SECURITY MEN: Arrangements have been made to have a sufficient number of Security Men and Policemen on duty all during the Senator's stay. Two Security Men will be on duty in front of the Senator's suite. No one is to be admitted to this suite without proper approval.

DOORMEN: Three doormen will be on duty at all times.

Pekin, Illinois.

BELLMEN: Full staff of bellmen on duty at all times; this totals twelve men.

(Also detailed are eating facilities, room service, laundry and valet, and medical services.)

As the campaign's heat mounted, I grew conscious of the abuse that a Presidential candidate is subjected to. I am referring not only to his heavy schedule, but to the ever-present hecklers. After a while, we were living on nervous energy. And our tempers were short—all except Kennedy's. If I had been asked for the eighth time in one morning, "Can a Catholic be President?," I'd have been tempted to reply, "I've answered that question seven times already! Do I have to repeat it?" or "You can look up the answer I gave in Springfield." But he maintained an outward appearance of freshness under the most adverse conditions—and he was never brusque or tactless.

The religious issue never ceased to haunt the campaign. It seemed to me that just when it was on the verge of dying down, somebody would fan the flames by making a ringing statement

deploring bigotry—thus reviving the issue. Nixon even charged that "the Kennedy camp is attempting to exploit the religious issue to solidify what they regard as 'a Catholic vote.'" And Harry Truman said in Seattle: "One of the saddest things about this whole sorry business is that some of the activity is carried on through our Protestant churches with political money contributed for the purpose to avoid paying income taxes."

John Kennedy was always kept informed. The hub of the Kennedy operation was his trusty Convair, the *Caroline*. Once aloft, the Senator would dictate to secretaries. In the rear of the cabin was a table at which Ted Sorensen and three brilliant speech writers—John Bartlow Martin, Richard Goodwin, and Joe Kraft—worked on the Senator's imminent talks. Theirs was frustrating labor, for Kennedy was likely to deliver only the first three minutes of his prepared speech. Then he would roll up his text and bang it for emphasis while he launched into an impromptu speech. The press found it dangerous to file stories written from the advance speeches; most newsmen hedged their accounts with this dis-

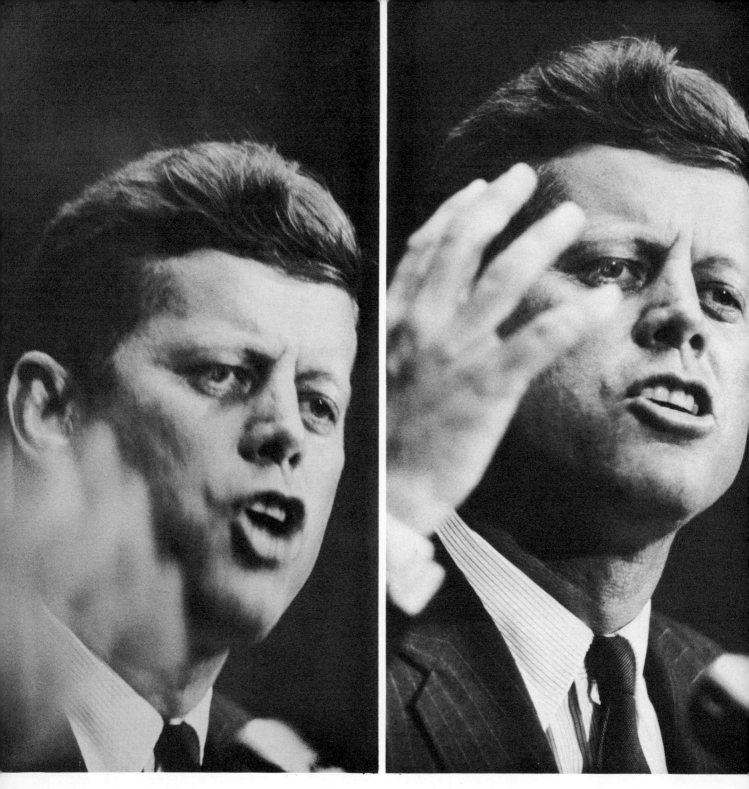

Senator Kennedy at Des Moines, Iowa, farm rally.

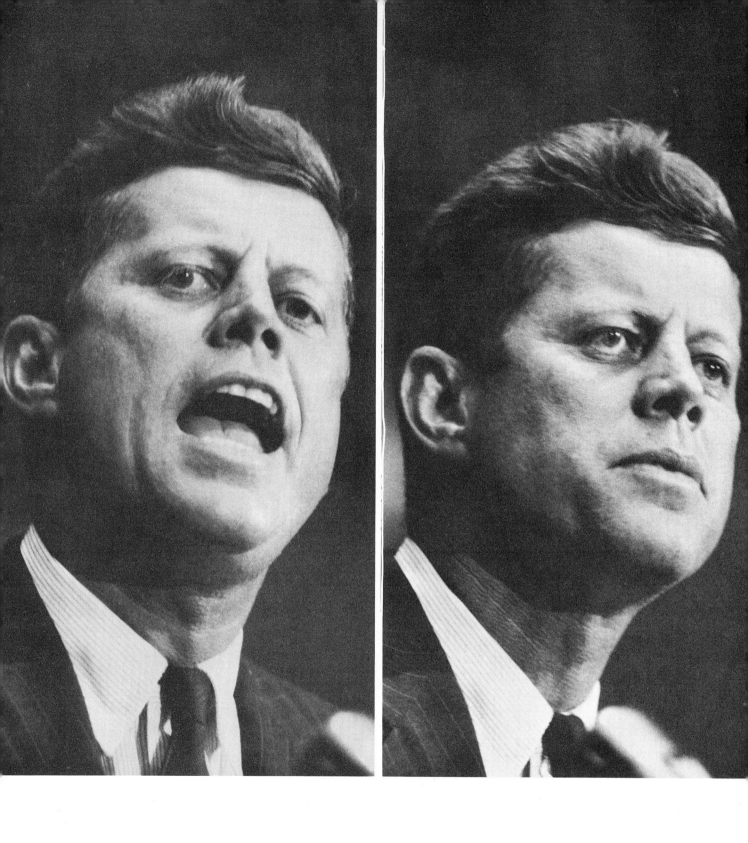

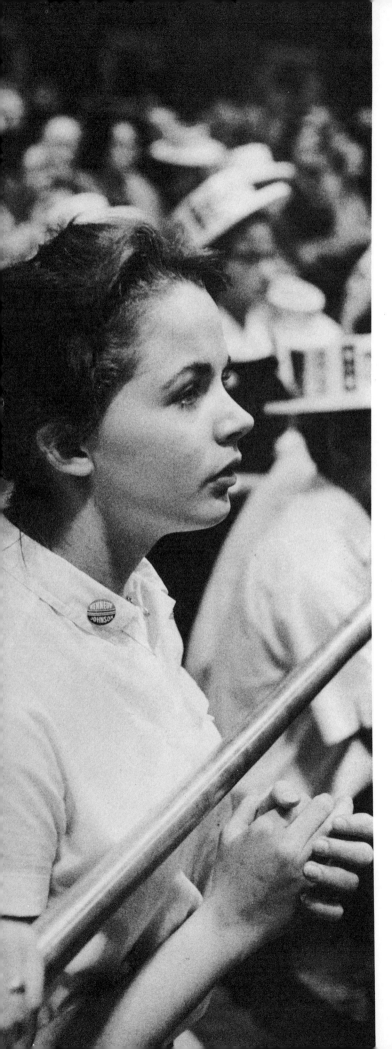

claimer: "Senator Kennedy, in a speech prepared for delivery at . . ."

On the press plane, there were a bar and bartender and two stewardesses and a festive spirit. There were always interesting strangers, some of whom I suspect were hitchikers who liked to travel in style. The food, when available, was palatable enough, but often there was none, except when the stewardesses replenished the larder with their own purchases. However, there was always an abundant supply of liquor aboard —and it was abundantly consumed. Occasionally, for lack of more solid fare, we had Scotch highballs for breakfast. On land we were kept so busy photographing official luncheons and other repasts, that we had no time to partake of the meals.

The crowds continued to swell. The Senator was having a curious effect on people. It was a mixture of personal magnetism and adulation. It started with women of all ages. In September, at an airport in upstate New York, a thirty-year-old blonde in a red sweater and checkered skirt broke through the police lines and planted a kiss on Senator Kennedy's cheek. She was the mother of three children, the youngest of whom was sitting in a stroller watching Mommie realize the American Dream, Women's Division. In Ohio, Governor Mike Di Salle had his coat ripped when he tried to protect the candidate for President from a crowd of grasping women. In a similar incident at Buffalo, Erie County Democratic chairman Peter J. Crotty had his pants torn by female manhandlers. A sixteen-year-old who couldn't get within reach of Kennedy shouted to a more fortunate friend, "Touch him for me, Gladys!"

After a while the men began to feel some of the candidate's appeal, too. Crowds would be silent when he began his speech, but the minute he smiled his audience began to shriek. Kennedy would end his talk by asking his listeners to give him their help. This would set them afire. Where Adlai Stevenson used to leave his audiences murmuring, "Great speech!," Jack Kennedy would leave them crying, "Let's march!" "Give me your help!" brought out all the maternal and paternal feelings a youngster can arouse. But the content of the speeches reminded his listeners that this was a statesman addressing them.

It was the second time in 1960 that I had wit-

162

nessed mass adulation. The first time was at the Stevenson demonstration in Los Angeles. I considered that one slightly hysterical. The Kennedy phenomenon was, in a way, quite different. And the Senator could be trusted to use his power wisely. But what if some unscrupulous demagogue ever attained this kind of hold on people?

At times Kennedy couldn't even put his program across because of the uproar. Sometimes, however, as in Hamtramck, Michigan, people stood in perfect silence while he spoke. They didn't scream. They didn't shout. They didn't whisper. And it wasn't hostility; it bordered on reverence. This was particularly the case where there were minority or immigrant populations. They had come to see a great American, who, they felt, cared about them and their problems. It was Franklin D. Roosevelt's appeal to the "common man" all over again.

People carried all sorts of signs. PUT THE MOXIE BACK IN DEMOCRACY is one that had to be explained to me. The campaign song was "Walking to Washington." I could see that all our people were thinking of just that.

In Iowa an old lady, with a face that was a photographer's dream, stood at a farm rally where Kennedy, Johnson, and Hubert Humphrey were the featured speakers. I took her picture and then asked what I could do for her.

"I want to see that Jack Kennedy. He's a wonderful young man," she told me.

"He's still inside getting ready," I said. "But Senator Humphrey's standing over there. He's a very important Senator down in Washington and he ran against Kennedy in Wisconsin and West Virginia."

"Where? Where?" she asked.

I called Senator Humphrey over and told him, "Senator, there's a lady here who would like to meet you."

Humphrey, who is always interested in shaking a hand, was glad to oblige. But my wonderful old lady asked him, "Just who are you, young man?"

"I'm Hubert Humphrey and I'm very pleased to meet you," he said.

"I didn't come here to see you," she told him sharply. "I came to see that Jack Kennedy, that wonderful man!" At this point I bowed out discreetly.

163

In Hamtramck, Michigan, this crowd of Polish and Slovak extraction listens to Kennedy's speech with rapt attention.

Some young girls watched and waited in silent rapture. And when Kennedy actually came near them, they often burst into tears. Traveling with him, I became aware of the great number of women in politics. There were many among the Volunteers for Kennedy, but nobody had time for romance. Many names and addresses were exchanged, however.

Except during the Great Debates on television, we seldom came face to face with the enemy. But at several airports we encountered the Republican "Truth Squad"—a team of Senators who followed Kennedy around with their version of the facts. Once they got slightly ahead of schedule and turned up in town before us. They spoke to an audience that was waiting for Kennedy, and answered his speech before he had even delivered it. But they didn't diminish the enthusiasm that greeted his arrival a few minutes later.

There were all sorts of lobbyists in the crowds. STEVENSON FOR SECRETARY OF STATE, many signs demanded. But Kennedy wasn't appointing his Cabinet before the votes were counted. "If I'm elected," he would answer, "I hope Governor Stevenson can play an important role in my administration." Other pressure groups had such ominous messages as COEXISTENCE OR NO EXISTENCE and WORLD PEACE OR WORLD DEATH. Hat salesmen also dogged our route. They were irritated by the Senator's bareheaded rides through blustery weather. Every now and then he obliged them by donning a hat—briefly.

In the technique of winning votes Kennedy employed many of the lessons learned in Boston ward politics. In fact, the first praetorian guard of his troops answered to the names of O'Brien, O'Donnell, O'Gorman, McGuire, Donahue, and Powers—all good Bostonian stalwarts. On the national level no wakes, baptisms, or weddings were attended. But the old politicians' habit of remembering everyone's name and making sure that everyone received personal thank-you notes was probably used on a national scale for the first time.

Kennedy's own campaign style was so sophisticated and dignified as to lift it far above the level of ward politics. There was no baby-kissing or posing in ten-gallon hats or Indian feathers, if he could help it. In fact, he was constantly

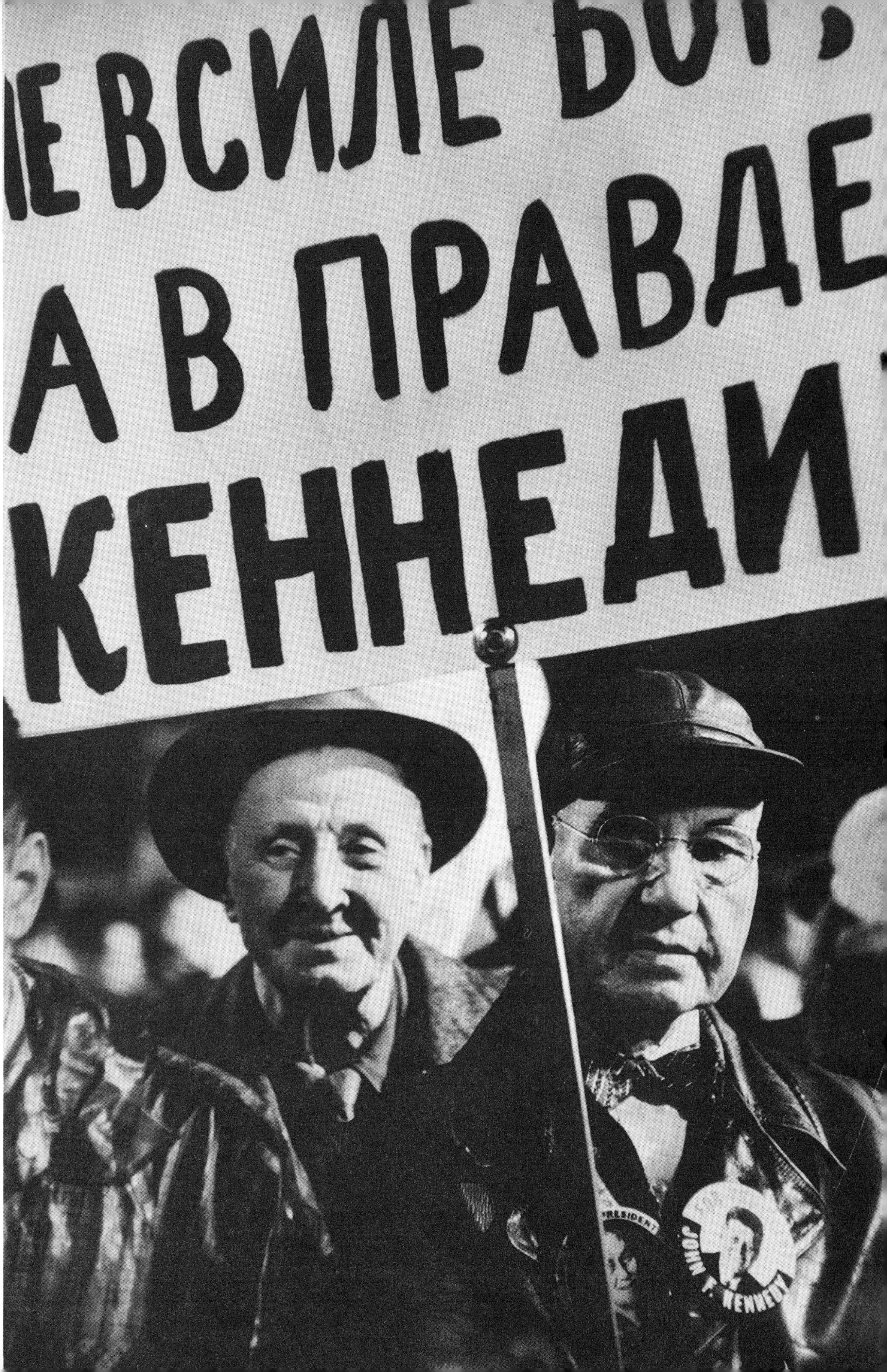
ВСИЛЕ
А В ПРАВДЕ
КЕННЕДИ
PRESIDENT
JOHN F. KENNEDY

The Kennedy-Nixon debates.
From left: Lee Radziwill (sister
of Mrs. Kennedy), Jacqueline,
Robert Kennedy, Kenneth
O'Donnell, watching third
debate in house especially
erected by the American
Broadcasting Company on the
set in New York.

resisting local efforts to include Democratic donkeys at political rallies.

His quotations from the classics, from history and poetry—especially from his favorite New England poet, Robert Frost—were apt and to the point, rather than used for sheer display of learning. However, because of the many speeches he had to make—as many as twenty daily—and because some ran no longer than ten minutes, a certain redundancy was bound to occur. The traveling press corps which had heard such phrases as "I think this country is ready to move again," or Robert Frost's famous lines "I have promises to keep./And miles to go before I sleep," over and over again began to paraphrase these quotes. Even the candidate got tired of some of the inevitable repetitions. And in a story he told about a certain Colonel Davenport, a historic political figure whose devotion to duty had been exemplary, Kennedy occasionally substituted the name of a traveling newsman, such as Colonel Alsop, Colonel Childs, or Colonel Reston. This joke was always good for a laugh among the press corps, even if it didn't immediately get across to his audience.

He developed into a good storyteller, too. He liked to tell his listeners about the governor who had a good record and was his party's standard-bearer. His audiences, conscious of the Catholic issue, assumed he was discussing Al Smith—particularly when Kennedy referred to the governor's disastrous defeat when he ran for the Presidency. But then he would end his story by saying, deadpan: "I am referring, of course, to Alf Landon, who opposed Roosevelt in 1936. And nobody ever said, Ladies and Gentlemen, that a Protestant couldn't be elected President."

He also told his audiences facetiously that a survey of American mothers revealed that some seventy per cent wanted their sons to grow up to be President of the United States—but only ten per cent wanted them to get there via politics.

In the course of the campaign I saw enough confetti to bury the White House. But I think confetti is one of the healthier trademarks of American politics. After a candidate has been deluged with confetti, it's rather hard for him to make a rabble-rousing speech, which would just seem out of place at a party.

Senator Kennedy never has been a rabble-rouser, of course, but he came a long way as an orator in the course of the 1960 campaign. He started out at about the same level that he had finished the primaries—literate, occasionally inspirational, generally mild-mannered, occasionally obscure. He talked too fast. Particularly in the Midwest, people couldn't understand what he was saying. His "pahk the cah in the Hahvard yahd" accent was distracting. But during the campaign, he was coached in voice projection and began to "Americanize" his inflections. He learned how to speak more slowly and to conserve his vocal resources. Even so, he was afflicted by an occasional sore throat.

But as his debate with Nixon (whom he privately respected) became more serious, his presentation grew more effective. His facial expressions became those of a crusader, his stance that of a fighter. For the first time, I was shooting action pictures of him. His detachment was vanishing. He had become concerned and his concern was contagious.

There had always been warmth in his crowds, but often it seemed to be warmth that his audiences brought to him. Now it was a two-way street. The Senator was breathing fire. He called Nixon a "leap-year liberal." "The Republican elephant," he said, "is like a circus elephant. It has a head full of ivory, a long memory, but no vision. And it travels in circles . . . and grabs the tail of the elephant in front."

He developed his flair for drama. Heading for Niagara Airport, he first had his pilot circle the Falls. But upon landing, he told the crowd: "The honeymoon is over."

Even in bad weather, he would always ride with the top down on his convertible wherever he saw a group of more than a few people. We always rode one car ahead in the motorcade—to photograph him coming forward.

One day we were on the road in a pouring rain. We stopped for a moment and the Senator's car pulled up alongside.

Kennedy came over to the photographers' car and inquired: "Would you guys mind riding in my car while I ride in yours?

When we agreed, he explained why: "My top doesn't open."

So he rode through the rain in our auto with the top down. The only person who complained about the swap of cars was Kennedy's first driver. The drivers were volunteers, and it was considered a great honor to chauffeur Kennedy around, an honor usually handed to especially hard workers or especially heavy contributors.

The first Great Debate, on Monday evening, September 26, 1960, between Richard M. Nixon and John F. Kennedy was the turning point of the campaign. Nixon's argument that Kennedy was a callow youth applying for a man's job was shattered by the Senator's mature grasp of the issues, as displayed to the television camera. And Kennedy pointed out: "The Vice-President and I came to the Congress together in 1946. We both served in the Labor Committee. I've been there now for fourteen years, the same period of time that he has, so that our experience in government is comparable." But as the two men grappled with American policy there was no comparison. Nixon could only echo, "clarify," or quibble.

The night of the first debate I was driving to Boston to photograph another Kennedy activity. During that summer session of Congress the Kennedy Foundation had been unjustly attacked and I was asked to document its charitable work. I heard the debate on the radio, free from the visual impact of television. In those terms I was convinced of Kennedy's victory, but listening later to a panel of newspapermen analyzing the debate I felt that they had watched the wrong Monday night fight, and the press summaries the next day reinforced this impression.

Many newspapers called the initial debate a "draw." *The Christian Science Monitor* said: "Both candidates measured up well in a difficult test. Both displayed poise, earnestness, keen intelligence, a vigorous grasp of national problems and a considered approach to solutions." "It must have produced, for non-partisans, a favorable impression of both candidates," said the *Bulletin,* which nearly everybody in Philadelphia reads. "A decorous draw," said the *Miami Herald.* "We should not say that anybody won. ... They both looked pretty young to us," commented the *St. Louis Post Dispatch.* And the *Richmond News Leader* thought that Nixon had won. It remained for James Reston of the *New York Times* to say in his column that the myth of immaturity had exploded and that Kennedy gained.

The public opinion polls that followed this debate shed no great light either. The only direct

Kennedy, with his sisters, answers the Nixon telethon on the day before election from Manchester, New Hampshire.

switch attributable to the debate, according to one newspaper poll, was a Negro janitor in Topeka, Kansas, formerly for Nixon, now for Kennedy. But what can be said is that an incredible number of Americans watched the debate. Later estimates ranged from 85 to 120 million viewers for one or all debates, and the Gallup polls finally established Kennedy as having been the winner.

The rest of the debates clearly didn't have the impact of the first. Nixon regained some lost ground and there was the first real clash on issues over the islands of Quemoy and Matsu. The third debate I remember particularly because of Nixon's reference to Harry Truman's bad campaign language. Later, at the Alfred E. Smith memorial dinner in New York, Senator Kennedy commented: "One of the inspiring notes that was struck in the last debate was struck by the Vice President in his very moving warning to the children of the nation and the candidates against the use of profanity by Presidents and ex-Presidents when they are on the stump." Then he said he didn't want people to think that "I am taking former President Truman's use of language lightly. I have sent him the following wire. 'Dear Mr. President: I have noted with interest your suggestion as to where those who vote for my opponent should go. While I understand and sympathize with your deep motivation, I think it is important that our side try to refrain from raising the religious issue.' "

The fourth debate was held in New York. The American Broadcasting Company had built for each candidate a little house on the set, to enable their friends and advisers to come and join them on the spot. Jacqueline made one of her rare appearances that day. She watched the screen tensely, as did her sister Lee, Robert Kennedy, and everybody else who was present.

When the debate ended, Kennedy came back and everybody shouted words of encouragement. But Jacqueline walked over to him and said softly, "You looked wonderful, Jack."

He quickly responded to her compliment. "You think so?" he asked her. "Do you really think so?" And when he saw that she did, all the tension went from his face. He put his arm around her and they walked off—a couple alone for the moment in their private world. And I had caught a glimpse of what there is between Mr. and Mrs. John F. Kennedy: a rare gift of communicating in a gesture or a sentence even when the pressures of their lives tend to keep them apart.

In the final days of the campaign we returned to New England. On the Monday before election Nixon presided at a four-hour telethon over ABC in a last effort to stem the tide.

In a half-hour telecast from a small studio in Manchester, New Hampshire, Senator Kennedy, surrounded by his sisters and Governor Hodges, tried to fight the onslaught.

On Election Eve we returned for a grand finale at the Boston Garden. All the politicians were there, but it was not a political event so much as a party. The big arena was packed with merrymakers. The narrow streets of Boston were impassable as the crowds engulfed our motorcade.

There was no need to analyze Kennedy's appeal any more. In Boston it wasn't paternal, maternal, or anything else, in fact.

In his campaign for the Presidency a native son had brought glory to the state of Massachusetts. Boston was proud of John Fitzgerald Kennedy. Senator Kennedy said that night, in his last speech of the campaign (from Faneuil Hall in Boston): "Our work is now over and tomorrow you must make your judgment."

The result of that final judgment, however, was to be held back until almost two days later.

175

Election— a day in limbo

John and Jacqueline Kennedy voted at 8:43 a.m. on Tuesday, November 8, 1960, in the basement of the West End Branch Library. He gave his address as Bowdoin Street. Although no electioneering is permitted near the polls, well-wishers came as close as they could, brandishing signs: WARD FIVE WELCOMES JACK, and THE LANDSLIDE STARTS HERE. One sign-carrier addressed herself to the candidate's wife: JACKIE, WE HOPE IT'S A BOY. Jacqueline Kennedy, wearing a purple coat and a leather beret, seemed amused and touched by this sign.

The out-of-towners traveling with Kennedy had already voted by absentee ballot. The day before had been a grueling one marked by huge, noisy crowds from Providence through Hartford to Boston. At the Boston Garden that night the noise had become inhuman, with frantic fans bobbing up and down in the hall. Kennedy, surrounded by an endless number of politicians and his family, had been able only to stand there and wave. It seemed as though the entire campaign had been compressed into one evening.

Back at the hotel I had watched Kennedy's final speech from Salinger's room, where a reluctant and tired Pierre found himself playing host to twenty or more newsmen who had come to ask a question and stayed. Everyone was exhausted but few could go to sleep. Yet at 7:30 this morning all had been ready for this decisive day.

After voting, the Kennedys flew to Cape Cod in the *Caroline,* to wait out the election; we traveled in another plane. John Kennedy carried a sheaf of telegrams that had been sent to him on this important day. VAYA CON DIOS (*Go with God*), said one. MAY GOD HELP YOU

Robert and Ethel Kennedy vote in Hyannis, Massachusetts.

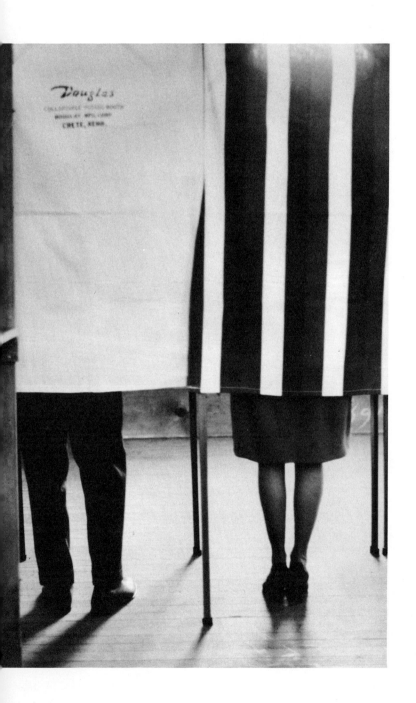

AND YOUR COUNTRY, implored another, signed, "Former Captain of Soviet Army." Said a third wire: DEAR JUVENILE JACK: GOD HELP OUR COUNTRY IF YOU ARE ELECTED. Kennedy himself was in a jovial mood. He inquired about Pierre Salinger's future plans and then remarked to Pierre: "You may be out job-hunting, you know."

At the airport in Hyannis, I buttonholed Kennedy to clean up an urgent piece of business that had been deferred for some time. The permanent photographers on his campaign swings had wanted a picture of themselves posing with the candidate. But nobody had stood still long enough for anyone to take a group shot. Today, however, the gang was all here. I decided that it was now or never. Election Day is the worst time to ask a politician for a favor; everyone's mind is racing ahead. But I told Kennedy that morning, "Senator, we've got to get that picture of the photographers."

"All right," he said. "Let's do it right now." Then we all gathered around him in the middle of a heaving sea of people while another photographer took the picture.

Then we piled into cars and made the ten-minute drive to the Senator's home, a curiously quiet drive. There were no cheering people along the road. The press had been diverted somewhere along the way and only the photo car followed the Senator, without taking a single picture. JFK's car top was down but he was no longer campaigning. The house was surrounded by police and in the brilliant sunshine a few tourists were hanging about. But there was no sign whatever of the roaring campaign that had taken place or of the historic day this was. It might have been any Tuesday, anywhere in New England with the ocean a few feet off and a few sailboats cruising lazily along. It was an altogether deceptive setting. I left to find my room at the Yachtsman, a local inn.

That morning, in fact most of the day, was unnaturally lazy. I went to the polls to get some local color and see Bob and Ethel Kennedy voting (Barnstable township, where Hyannis Port is situated, would go heavily Republican, as it had in all the years before). Later that morning all photographers present went out to get a picture of JFK and his family. Aside from this there was nothing to do but eat, drink and sleep a little.

Activity began about six that evening. A pool had been chosen and we went out to the Kennedy Compound to start our long vigil.

John Kennedy's house on Irving Avenue in Hyannis Port is a white eight-room clapboard-and-shingle house with green shutters. You have to pass by it to get to the pier, which is about 400 feet down the road. The house is sheltered on the road side by a high wooden fence, but completely open from the back. It looks across a beautiful lawn at Robert's somewhat larger house. And from there it is but a hundred feet to the "big house," the Ambassador's house, which is the largest of the three and commands a magnificent view of Nantucket Sound. For years, old Nantucket ferryboat captains have pointed out this house standing at the very edge of the Sound. These three houses form an irregular triangle with their backs facing each other. There is a tennis court and a children's carousel on the green and from Joseph P. Kennedy's house a gentle lawn descends toward the dunes; beyond that lies the beautiful white-sand beach of the Cape.

This is the setting in which we were to wait throughout the night for America to decide who

was going to be the next President, and here with us was one of the principals.

By the time we arrived at the Kennedy home the nation's papers had already had their headlines. Hart's Location in New Hampshire had been the first hamlet to report, giving 8 votes to Kennedy and 4 to Nixon. There had been a lot of other hot news, Kennedy had won in Nixon, New Jersey, and Nixon had conquered Kennedy, New York. For the rest the television commentators talked mainly about what the computers were going to do and explained them to a country that was not yet really listening. Alabama, Indiana, Mississippi, and Vermont had already closed their polls. But no results anywhere near complete were in yet.

Back at the Armory, as we left, activity had begun to mount. The Hyannis National Guard Armory had been set up as press headquarters and it was here that Senator Kennedy was expected to arrive this evening—either as the President-elect or as the defeated candidate. The room was a maze of cameras, telephones, and typewriters. Pierre Salinger and his deputy Don Wilson presided, giving infrequent bulletins on what the Senator was doing. The 200-plus members of the press were wandering aimlessly around and the photographers early in the day had marked spots by name and publication on the long, wooden platform facing the dais. Everyone was ready.

Many of these men and women had covered all or most of the campaign and many of them, in contrast with their editors and publishers, were fervent Kennedy supporters. Their hope was that Kennedy would come out early, to meet the morning deadlines, and that he would come out a winner.

But before that could happen one blow had to

be digested. One of the infernal, all-knowing IBM computers that the commentators shortly before had so fondly introduced as "man's best friend," now came through with its first prediction. On the basis of carefully fed information, taking all the facts of voting into account, it now told us that Nixon was the 100–1 winner, and that he would carry 459 electoral votes as against 78 for Kennedy. I remember being rather shocked by this at first, then shrugging it off as sheer nonsense. But the worry brought on by this prediction never quite left me during the night. In retrospect I am quite happy about the prediction. It is, it seems to me, one of the few recent victories of man over machine.

By now, a command post, at Robert Kennedy's house was in full swing. I remember well the scene when we entered the house to take our first pictures. Going in by the back door, the scene was great bedlam. About twenty men and women, dressed in slacks, sports clothes, or business suits were watching a huge TV set in the opposite corner. Some were conversing in hushed tones. Singer Morton Downey, a friend of Joseph P.'s, was going around offering sandwiches and coffee. All here were friends and relatives, cousins and nephews and nieces, supporters and campaign workers, now without a job to do.

Crossing the large living room, one reached a sun porch which opened up to the left through large paneled glass doors on the dining room. The porch, usually cluttered with toys, tonight had been set up as a telephone center in a sort of T formation, the bar of the T facing the dining room. Fourteen telephones connected to nerve centers around the country and telling how key districts were voting were manned there. The girls—Pamela Turnure, Pauline Fluit, Helen

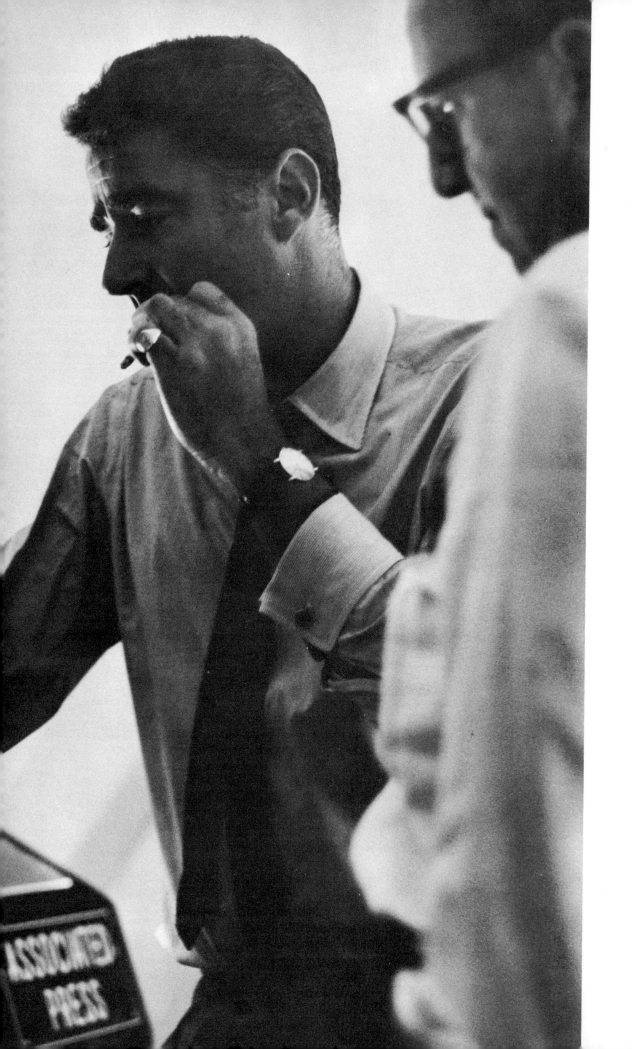

Lempart, Judy Hackett—all were veterans of the campaign and at the head of the table Kenny O'Donnell, Larry O'Brien and occasionally Robert Kennedy would immediately evaluate the reports or get them upstairs to a second room. Jim Williams, an AT&T vice-president who had managed the communications system throughout the campaign, was there to make sure of technical efficiency.

Upstairs, in the children's bedrooms, now all cleared of furniture, the major planning and evaluation took place. Steve Smith and Ted Kennedy sat in front of a table, across from a portable TV, cluttered with papers full of charts and numbers. The girls, Ethel Kennedy, Pat Lawford, and Eunice Shriver, all dressed in bright slacks, were holding ballots and comparing notes.

Joan Kennedy, Teddy's wife, was on the telephone, trying to collect a small bet she had made with a close Republican friend, who had worked hard for Nixon, but refused to pay off at this time.

From the wall the picture of a clown was staring down at the proceedings, reminding all that this was normally the room of Kathleen Kennedy, oldest daughter of the campaign manager.

In a third room on that same floor the real nerve center was functioning. Here analyst Lou Harris was working, comparing, evaluating, deciding. Ben Smith was assisting, so was Dave Hackett; Bobby Kennedy was bouncing in and out. From here, too, bulletins went to the Armory and out around the country with specific instructions.

Out in the hall, wire-service tickers had been set up and Peter Lawford was nervously ripping the sheets off as soon as they got long enough to tear.

My pictures of that evening show two different moods in all this. One, taken around midnight, shows the girls, at least, in gay party spirit. JFK then showed a popular lead of over 2,000,000

The activity at the Robert Kennedy house and the Armory in Hyannis. The JFK house (lower right) *was lit up well, inside and out, until shortly before 4 a.m.*

votes. And later on that same group, as our margin got smaller and smaller, seems worried and almost forlorn.

The candidate remained in seclusion for most of that evening at his own house. As soon as darkness had fallen TV networks had set up their lights illuminating the house now, giving the effect of an empty movie set. Inside we could see the lights burning in the living room, and every once in a while the Senator would walk across the lawn to visit his brother Bobby's house.

At around midnight he walked across once more, to remain for the rest of the night.

By this time the news on television was changing slowly but surely. Having reached a high point, shortly after midnight, of a 2,300,000 popular lead, the trend now slowly reversed. The early lead had been built up mainly by Connecticut, Pennsylvania, and New York, but now the figures shown on the screen were from the Midwest and the Far West.

The television calculators, which had earlier predicted a Nixon landslide, had by now changed their mechanical minds, but the popular vote nevertheless kept going down and down. Now the major commentators, calling on other commentators, were giving their predictions and only adding to the confusion: *Kennedy is going to make it . . . he'll win the electoral vote but lose the popular vote . . . he'll loose by a slight margin.*

Somehow or other I knew we were going to make it that night—or was it just wishful thinking? In 1956 I was convinced Stevenson would win; all logic pointed to it yet he lost by a landslide. Was it going to happen again? All the various Kennedys would say was that we weren't losing, but we weren't winning either. If it was to be a draw, the unpledged Southern electors would decide the election, and they, from all I knew, were unsympathetic to Kennedy.

The most perplexing states were Ohio and Wisconsin. It was impossible to believe that these were the same states in which huge crowds had cheered the Senator. Wisconsin—where he

With the election still undecided, the family gathers in Ambassador Kennedy's house. The time is 10:30 on Wednesday morning.

had handed Hubert Humphrey his first defeat, where Kennedy was practically an adopted son! And Ohio—where his welcome from town to town had been nothing short of triumphant. And on the West Coast some bad mistakes had very obviously been made. But none of them had shown up during the campaign swings.

Back at the Armory, the newsmen were pressuring Pierre Salinger for an appearance of Senator Kennedy, and everyone was waiting for Nixon to concede, for in spite of the slow decline of the popular-vote lead Kennedy kept gaining electoral votes.

About 3 a.m. Eastern time, word came that Nixon would put in an appearance at the ballroom of the Ambassador Hotel in Los Angeles.

At this point, even the White House staff got its signals crossed. Presidential Press Secretary James Hagerty assumed that Nixon would concede. Hagerty dispatched a congratulatory telegram that President Eisenhower had authorized him to send to Kennedy if Nixon lost.

There was an endless wait—and then word that Nixon *wasn't* coming down. Then he did come down, accompanied by his wife Pat, who was crying. He thanked his supporters rather formally, but he wasn't conceding yet.

It took Jim Hagerty and Western Union thirty frantic minutes to intercept the President's telegram before it could be delivered in Hyannis Port.

In a statement interrupted by shouts of *"We want Nixon!"* and *"You're still the best man!"* Nixon declared at 3:30 a.m.:

"I am sure that many are listening here who are supporting Mr.—Senator Kennedy. I know too that he probably is listening to this program.

"And while the—and I—please, please, just a minute—and I—as I look at the board here: while there are still some results still to come in —if the present trend continues, Mr.—Senator Kennedy will be the next President of the United States."

Looking back on it, Nixon's behavior was sportsmanlike and downright heroic: Americans wouldn't want a President who gave up too hastily. And there was still hope for Nixon: Kennedy's lead in Illinois had declined from 200,000 to 50,000; in California, Kennedy led by fewer than 100,000 votes. The Senator's lead in the popular vote was below a million—less than half what it had been a few hours ago.

But as we watched Nixon on television with the attention that is given a particularly good drama, all we could think was that Nixon had some nerve postponing our victory. Why would he prolong the agony? We were far more impatient than impartial.

The campaign workers in the command center were, of course, just as furious and the press clamored again for a Kennedy appearance. But Senator Kennedy sent word that he wasn't going to make a statement until Nixon came out again. Pierre Salinger relayed his message to the press. Shortly before 4 a.m. the last light went out in the Senator's house.

I went to sleep on a cot in the maid's quarters of the estate. Twice I was awakened by people shouting, "He's conceded! He's conceded!" Each time it was a false alarm. The second time, I bolted off the cot, seized my camera, ran out the door and smack into a tree. After that, I was less enthusiastic.

By the time I awoke again—shortly after 7:30 a.m.—Secret Service men had arrived. This was a good omen, I thought. I was amazed at the efficiency of these men. They knew every authorized face, every authorized name, and although I slightly resented, at first, this wall of strangers coming now between the Senator and those who had worked so hard and faithfully for him, I had to admire their complete control. I think everybody in the Kennedy entourage felt a little this way.

Wednesday was another clear and beautiful day, and I went over to Bobby's house to try and get some coffee for the exhausted press corps. Ethel was alone downstairs in the communications center, now void of people and activity; only the telephones and some papers strewn about reminded one of the fever pitch the night before. Ethel was trying to tidy up a bit and I related my request. "The maids are all out," she said, "but why just coffee? Let's have breakfast." Ethel Kennedy marched to the stove and cooked breakfast for eleven guests. We had ham and eggs and hot rolls and good strong coffee, which we badly needed after that anxious night.

While we were at breakfast the family members, with Bobby—who had not gone to bed that night—were out on the beach for a long walk. They had to stretch their muscles and shake their exhaustion. Bobby carried a football but no one was in the mood to play.

Later on in the "big house" everyone assembled, including the Senator, sitting on the steps. Everything was still very tense; Nixon had yet to concede—and the popular vote kept sliding. "Lem" Billings, JFK's old friend who had been active in Wisconsin, was trying to puzzle out our defeat there. I tried to kid Lem, making a joke about his work there. He didn't take it well. "Is that supposed to be funny?" he asked, and I dropped the subject at once. Obviously, no one was celebrating yet.

Caroline Kennedy had gone riding that morning on her Irish pony, accompanied by her grandfather. She provided the one relief. When Mr. Kennedy had asked her what she had said to her daddy this morning she answered, "Good morning, Mr. President."

Shortly after 11 a.m. the Senator, with his brother and some in-laws, adjourned again to Bobby's house to continue watching television. Kennedy was still 11 votes short of the 269 required to win, but any minute now one of the big states—Illinois or Minnesota—would be decided and he was leading in both.

At 12:33 in the afternoon, Kennedy won Minnesota, which put him over. Twelve minutes later, Nixon sent a telegram to Hyannis Port: I WANT TO REPEAT THROUGH THIS WIRE THE CONGRATULATIONS AND BEST WISHES I EXTENDED TO YOU ON TELEVISION LAST NIGHT. I KNOW THAT YOU WILL HAVE THE UNITED SUPPORT OF ALL AMERICANS AS YOU LEAD THE NATION IN THE CAUSE OF PEACE AND FREEDOM IN THE NEXT FOUR YEARS.

Hearing this news on television, John F. Kennedy loosened his grip on a pencil that he had held tensely throughout the last hour. The whole family had been so wrapped up in the political struggle that they hadn't even noticed me taking pictures.

Kennedy replied to Nixon's telegram: I KNOW THAT THE NATION CAN CONTINUE TO COUNT ON YOUR UNSWERVING LOYALTY IN WHATEVER EFFORT YOU UNDERTAKE AND THAT YOU AND I CAN MAINTAIN OUR LONG-STANDING CORDIAL RELATIONS IN THE YEARS AHEAD.

193

There was a similar exchange of telegrams with Dwight Eisenhower, and the rest all seemed anticlimactic.

Jacqueline Kennedy described the period between the closing of the polls and the moment of victory as "the longest night in history." Now she seemed dazed as people rushed up to congratulate her. After a while, she donned her raincoat and went for a solitary walk along the beach. She had been cast in the role of First Lady and now she began composing herself for it.

In Bobby's living room the scene had changed remarkably. Finally there was certainty and the long struggle was over. A sigh of relief was almost audible and all got up and walked into the sun room, where they stood with bright

smiles looking up at their brother. Then John Kennedy asked for his wife and he went down to the beach to find her. While Jacqueline went in to dress for a picture and get ready to go to the Armory, John F. Kennedy went for a long walk with Caroline.

My first conversational encounter with John F. Kennedy as President-elect was in his father's house. Schutzer, Tretick, and I walked in and the Senator saw us from the next room. We smiled at each other and then John Kennedy jumped up and came across the room with outstretched hands. "How are you doing, Jacques?" I remember him saying. I was full of emotion, almost unable to speak, and through my mind flashed the question of what to call him now. I finally managed to say: "Congratulations Mr. President." He laughed. In fact, he seemed a little flustered. Then he said, "Thanks a lot."

After this there was a great confusion as to whether there was time to get a family picture or not, but finally all were in place except Jacqueline Kennedy. When she arrived, Senator

The acceptance speech in the Hyannis Armory, and two important onlookers, Kennedy's brother and father.

Kennedy went to the door to escort her in; and then suddenly the entire family spontaneously applauded as the two of them joined the group. It was a beautiful moment and the family's way of showing their complete devotion. Only then did it really bear in on me completely that John F. Kennedy was President now.

At 1:30 p.m. the entire family made the victorious trek to the Armory, where the press was waiting. There was one sad interlude along the way. The family's chauffeur, who had been in their employ since John Kennedy was a young boy, wanted to drive the next President on this triumphant occasion. This was the biggest day in the chauffeur's life. But Secret Service won't allow anyone except its own men to drive the President. Kennedy spoke up for the chauffeur, but Secret Service overruled him. The chauffeur ended up driving behind the Presidential car— with Joseph Kennedy to console him. John Kennedy was beginning to realize that the President of the United States is, in many ways, public property.

Kennedy's Armory speech was straightforward and characteristic. After saying that this was "a satisfying moment to me" and thanking his supporters, he added: "To all Americans I say that the next four years are going to be difficult and challenging years for us all. The election may have been a close one, but I think that there is general agreement by all of our citizens that a supreme national effort will be needed in the years ahead to move this country safely through the nineteen-sixties."

He concluded: "So now my wife and I prepare for a new administration and for a new baby. Thank you."

Although his statement was hardly emotional, the press had brought plenty of its own feeling into that flag-bedecked Armory. This was the end of a very sentimental journey for the newsmen who had covered the campaign.

Looking around the room there were many of America's greatest journalists, and all of John Kennedy's closest staff members. As the President-elect slowly made his way out of the Armory, shaking hands with newsmen and staffers, I could see tears on many of their faces. When I show some of them photos I took that day, they don't even recognize themselves.

The inauguration, 1961

My Washington hotel room was a bargain at $30 a day, even though its customary rate of $8.50 a day was considered high in more normal times. But this was a time like no other time—the inauguration of John Fitzgerald Kennedy as the thirty-fifth President of the United States.

I had arrived several days before Friday, January 20, 1961, and it was well that I did. I had to pick up credentials for every occasion. During the inaugural parade one pass would allow me to stand at 16th Street and Pennsylvania Avenue, but I would need another to shoot pictures at 14th and Pennsylvania. And I would have to get a third pass that would allow me to walk from 16th Street to 14th Street. Every credential was of a different color.

Soon after I arrived I was handed an official press document called "Brief Notes on the Inaugural Parade." It was 600 pages long, and contained authorized biographies of all participants in the floats, bands, and honor guards.

Those who had received and accepted handsomely engraved official invitations to the Inauguration found that their troubles were just beginning when they set foot in Washington. There were block-long lines of people trying to exchange invitations for tickets to each event. I never did get my tickets, although I had an invitation.

I finally received a staff badge marked ALL EVENTS, ALL AREAS and that I knew would

cover me, for in the two and a half months since Election Day, I had learned to appreciate Kennedy's Secret Service men and I knew badges finally meant something.

It was a grand reunion. Everyone who'd had anything to do with the campaign was there. People I'd met fleetingly in Oregon, Wisconsin, West Virginia, or New Hampshire turned up again, and the Mayflower lobby at all times seemed like a campaign who's who.

On the afternoon of Thursday the nineteenth, I set out to cover a rehearsal of the Inaugural Gala, the $100-a-seat spectacular produced by Frank Sinatra. When I arrived at the National Guard Armory at 1:30 p.m., it had just started to snow lightly. Later on that day I had planned to attend three more functions at which the President-elect was slated to appear. But I missed everything that day except the evening Gala.

After two hours of the rehearsal I left to go back to my hotel and change. But going outside, I found a blizzard had started and covered everything with eight inches of snow.

Luckily for me, a cab was discharging a passenger at the Armory, so I had transportation. The driver was worried when I told him I wanted to get to the Mayflower Hotel, where I had to cover another ceremony. "It's pretty bad out," he said, "and we may have trouble getting into town, but I'll give it a try."

This would normally have been a twenty-minute cab ride. After two hours in the same cab, I lost confidence in my driver and switched to another. The first cab had crawled for two hours; the second cab stood still for forty-five

Left : *The President-Elect and Mrs. Kennedy at the Armory Gala watch the performance of stellar talent, such as Gene Kelly* (right).

minutes. I then took a bus, which moved me five blocks in half an hour. Then I walked several blocks, and slowly saw the entire day pass by without a single picture.

It was almost eight o'clock when I arrived at the Mayflower, dressed in a sport jacket and bow tie. The Gala was to be a black-tie affair, but there had been no way to get back to my hotel; the blizzard had begun to immobilize Washington. This was definitely my worst crisis since the enraged photographer assaulted me in Peoria.

The elegant lobby of the Mayflower had become a displaced-persons camp. People in assorted degrees of dishevelment stood around confusing one another. Would the Gala be canceled or postponed or held on schedule? The blind were leading the blind.

I telephoned Pierre Salinger, who was on his way down; he was cheerful as ever. "I don't know what's going on," he said, "but let's try to make it out there." He offered me a ride in his brother's car, which had snow tires.

"But look at me," I said. "I can't go like this, can I?"

"Have it your way," Pierre responded. "You can stay or you can go. Do you want to go?" The answer was obvious, and we made it back in just under an hour. The Armory was empty when we arrived punctually at 10 p.m., but the Gala hadn't begun yet—and it didn't for quite a while. Slowly more people started arriving.

The formal-dress requirement had been waived by then. Some women came in evening dress, others in sport clothes. You simply wore the best

201

*The last few minutes on
N Street in Washington, D.C.*

you could find—and came as you were. Some of
the entertainers, too, had been estranged from
their wardrobes. Ethel Merman, for instance, sang
"Everything's Coming Up Roses" in her street
clothes.

The President-elect and his wife arrived
shortly before 11 p.m. in formal dress. Kennedy
had already been to the Inaugural Concert at
Constitution Hall. Only a few hundred people
had been there. Arriving at the Gala, he seemed
the most unperturbed man in town. A reporter
asked him, "Are you excited?"

Kennedy reflected for a moment and then said,
"Interested."

Herbert Hoover had been scheduled to attend
the festivities, but his Air Force DC-6 had
circled Washington for an hour and then returned to Miami when it couldn't land in the
snowstorm. The former President was in the
air almost ten hours.

The Gala proved to be Secret Service's first
inkling of the difficult job they would have
guarding the next President. He is fast-moving
and friendly. He came in, sat down, recognized
old friends, jumped up and started shaking
hands. He would disappear into the mob and
then reappear sporadically. I tried to follow him,
but I kept losing him and finding him. People
hurrying by kept asking me if I'd seen him. For
thirty minutes, none of us could find him. Someone thought of asking TV cameramen to focus
on the crowd and try to locate him. Even they
were unsuccessful. Finally, the President-elect
reappeared.

Leonard Bernstein struck up the overture, and
the show went on. It was a good show. Tony
Curtis and Janet Leigh, Joey Bishop, Gene Kelly,
Laurence Olivier, Frederic March, Pat Suzuki,

President-Elect and Mrs. Kennedy leave their Georgetown house for the White House to pick up President Eisenhower on the way to the swearing-in ceremony.

Ella Fitzgerald, and many more of America's best talent had made sacrifices to get here and performed without pay. Sinatra, who had produced the whole show, received an ovation and a special citation from the President-elect.

Getting back after the Gala was another problem. Travel in the city was still snarled, although the Sanitation Department had borrowed snow-removal equipment from the Army Engineers at Fort Belvoir, Virginia. It was, according to old Washingtonians, the worst inaugural weather since William Howard Taft had been sworn in fifty-two years earlier.

I fell into bed at 4:30 a.m. after leaving a call for six o'clock—and prayed the next day would be somewhat more successful.

I reached the Kennedys' home in Georgetown at 9 a.m. on Inauguration Day. The President-elect was at Mass and I went there to wait for him.

The snow had stopped falling, but the streets were piled high with huge mounds. The temperature was 22 and the winds were bitter. People stood across the narrow street from the church, shivering and staring.

Back at 3307 N Street, Kennedy had one neighborly gesture to perform before he left for the White House. It was his idea. During the "lame duck" period—between election and inauguration—he had announced his key appointments from the steps of his house. It was a long, cold winter and a compassionate lady, Miss Helen Montgomery, who lived across the street, had opened her doors to the freezing newsmen who waited outside for the latest bulletin. Soon her home became a maze of telephones and teletypes. She served her guests coffee and cookies and assorted jellies. As a reward for her meri-

torious service to American journalism, John Kennedy stopped in to present her a plaque on that eventful morning. He also arranged for a police escort to take his good neighbor to the swearing-in ceremonies.

"I know how much the reporters appreciated your hospitality," Kennedy told Miss Montgomery. "Even down in Florida, they wanted to come back here."

The genteel lady had tears in her eyes. "Senator, I'm overcome. I mean President-elect," she said emotionally. "Please forgive me. I am overcome."

Shortly after eleven o'clock speaker of the house, Sam Rayburn, and Senator John Sparkman arrived to escort the President-elect and his lady to the White House. There they were to pick up President and Mrs. Eisenhower to ride together to the swearing-in ceremony.

A few minutes later Kennedy, carrying his top hat, and Jacqueline drove off for the first time in a car bearing the Presidential seal. I rode in the photographers' car in front of them. At the White House, President Eisenhower came down the steps to meet the President-elect. Both men went inside. Shortly afterward, they emerged again. They were chatting amiably, posed a moment for photographers, and left in the bubble-top Presidential car.

This then was the orderly transfer of power in a democracy and I shall never forget it. Here, on the imposing portico of the White House stood the Thirty-fourth and the Thirty-fifth Presidents of the United States of America. One a distinguished soldier, a Republican Midwesterner from old farm stock, Protestant, a man well into his seventieth year; and Kennedy, thirty years his junior, third-generation American, Catholic, Democrat, urban son of great wealth. No two

men could be more different, yet both had been duly elected by the people of this great country. They were at this point surrounded by a hundred or so newsmen, staff, military, and security men. Television was recording the scene; the whole country, the whole world was watching.

In the stands outside the Capitol, it seemed one happy party. All the Kennedys were there. Jacqueline Kennedy wore a simple beige coat with a circlet fur collar and a matching pillbox headpiece; she carried a small mink muff. In the bright sun against a background of snow, the President-elect's father and mother positively shone.

President Eisenhower seemed very content and former President Truman particularly happy. Also in the first row sat Vice-President Nixon and his wife. In the Senator's gallery sat Hubert Humphrey and Stuart Symington and Eugene McCarthy. Adlai Stevenson was among the visitors, and among the faces of the old familiar staff and campaign workers could be seen the new men of the Cabinet. Everyone had come to pay tribute and see the new President sworn in. Beyond, in the glaring sunshine that was slowly melting the snow, face was next to face and a tree void of leaves this cold January day was black with people who had climbed up, trying to get a better look.

Into this setting came John F. Kennedy, solemn and dignified. If he had been gregarious and merry the night before, his mood was markedly different this morning. He was aware, as was everybody else present, of the making of history—of Washington, Jefferson, Adams, and Jackson; of all his predecessors; of the continuity of power, for John Kennedy is a man who loves history, who studies history, and is aware that he is making it.

Marian Anderson sang "The Star-Spangled Banner" and Cardinal Cushing of Boston began a lengthy prayer. Suddenly, Capitol guards and Secret Service men were kneeling on the red carpet where Cardinal Cushing stood. They were looking for the source of some wispy blue smoke that was drifting up from the lectern. The Cardinal continued and the kneelers soon traced the smoke to a short circuit.

Other prayers—by Archbishop Iakovos of the Greek Orthodox Church; Dr. John Barclay, pastor of Central Christian Church in Austin, Texas; and Rabbi Nelson Glueck, president of Hebrew Union College in Cincinnati—were far less spectacular.

At 12:40, Speaker Rayburn administered the Vice-Presidential oath to his fellow Texan, Lyndon Johnson.

Robert Frost, the eighty-six-year-old New England poet, had come to read his poem, "The Gift Outright," at the invitation of the President-elect. Frost struck me as an incredibly old man, as his white hair waved in the wind and his hands trembled while he unfolded his manuscript.

As a surprise, he had written a preface that was more than twice the length of the poem. In a quavering voice, he began to read:

"Summoning artists to participate
In the august occasions of the state
Seems something for us all to celebrate."

The wind lashed the edges of Frost's paper. Bright sun made his own words invisible to the elderly poet. "I am not having a good light here at all," Frost murmured unhappily. The surging spirit of this man, the poet at the affair of state—in effect this nation's poet laureate—and his great humility came through to everyone, and spontaneous applause broke the silence. The Vice-President tried to shade Frost's manuscript, but the poet waved him away.

"This was to have been a preface to a poem which I do not have to read," Frost told the gathering. Then he threw back his shoulders, straightened his head and declaimed in a firm voice:

"The land was ours before we were the land's,
 She was our land more than a hundred years.
 Before we were her people she was ours
 In Mississippi, in Virginia,
 But we were England's, still colonials,
 Possessing what we still were unpossessed by,
 Possessed by what we now no more possessed.
 Something we were withholding left us weak
 Until we found out that it was ourselves
 We were withholding from our land of living
 And forthwith found salvation in surrender.
 Such as we were we gave ourselves outright
 (The deed of gift was many deeds of war)
 To the land, vaguely realizing westward,
 But still unstoried, artless, unenhanced,
 Such as she was, such as she would become."

His eloquence made him seem stronger than young men. What a beautiful way this was to celebrate the occasion. John Kennedy jumped up to thank him and escort him back to his seat.

Now a hush fell as Chief Justice Warren intoned the oath of office and John Fitzgerald Kennedy, his left hand resting on an old family Bible, repeated after him: "I do solemnly swear that I will faithfully execute the office of President of the United States, and will, to the best of my ability, preserve, protect, and defend the Constitution of the United States."

Then the new President turned toward the people and began his Inaugural Address:

"Let the word go forth from this time and place, to friend and foe alike," he proclaimed, "that the torch has been passed to a new generation of Americans—born in this century, tempered by war, disciplined by a hard and bitter

*On the Inaugural stand, from
left and watching the parade,
Attorney General Robert F.
Kennedy, Supreme Court
Justices Clark, Frankfurter, and
Black, Treasury Secretary
Douglas Dillon, brother-in-law
and Director of the Peace Corps
Sargent Shriver.*

peace, proud of our ancient heritage—and unwilling to witness or permit the slow undoing of those human rights to which this nation has always been committed, and to which we are committed today at home and around the world."

I listened to his words with pride that I saw reflected in every face on that crowded platform and with awe that millions of Americans felt as they heard a familiar voice utter words of resounding greatness. President Kennedy spoke boldly to the whole world.

"In the long history of the world, only a few generations have been granted the role of defending freedom in its hour of maximum danger. I do not shrink from this responsibility—I welcome it. I do not believe that any of us would

216

exchange places with any other people or any other generation. The energy, the faith, the devotion which we bring to this endeavor will light our country and all who serve it—and the glow from that fire can truly light the world."

In the unnatural brightness of a chilly day, I gazed around the platform. Richard M. Nixon's face attracted my attention momentarily. There he was, just a few ironic feet away—so near and yet so far!

"And so, my fellow Americans," the President concluded, "Ask not what your country can do for you—ask what you can do for your country. My fellow citizens of the world: ask not what America will do for you, but what together we can do for the freedom of man.

"Finally, whether you are citizens of America or citizens of the world, ask of us here the same high standards of strength and sacrifice which we ask of you. With a good conscience our only sure reward, with history the final judge of our deeds, let us go forth to lead the land we love, asking His blessing and His help, but knowing that here on earth God's work must truly be our own."

After the Inauguration ceremony, elder statesman Dwight D. Eisenhower went to a private luncheon—without a motorcycle escort, a Secret Service chauffeur, or any of the trappings of eight years in the White House. Then he drove as a private citizen to his farm in Gettysburg, Pennsylvania.

John F. Kennedy could not know this seclusion for at least four years. Instead, he went in to a crowded luncheon in the old Supreme Court chamber of the Capitol building. There he signed the menu for hearty, seventy-six-year-old Harry Truman, at one time a strong opponent. I had troubles for the last time trying to get in and shoot—and Ted Kennedy once more bailed me out.

The drive up Constitution and Pennsylvania avenues from the Capitol to the White House was a slow, inspiring procession. The new President and his First Lady rode in an open car and the people, protected by boots against the slush and some wearing blankets against the cold, lined the streets solidly, five and six deep along the route.

Somewhere near the Treasury the Kennedy grandchildren had been given a special vantage point. As the car passed there, the new First Lady looked back and up, spotted the kids, smiled, waved, and beckoned to her husband, who also waved.

A truck had been provided for photographers to cover the Kennedys' slow progress, but it kept so far ahead that it was useless. I jumped off, and with twenty pounds of camera equipment strapped to me, intermittently stopping to take a picture, I trotted the entire distance through slush and snow, staying next to the President's car. It was exhausting, and the President, spotting me there a couple of times, waved across and shook his head.

I was so fatigued that I didn't realize when I reached the White House. I was stopped. But the family had asked me to come into the box and photograph from there. My name had been given and my credential number was registered at the gate.

The President entered the box in high spirits. It must have been about 3 p.m. He and Jac-

queline, the Vice-President and Lady Bird, immediately went to the front, there to stand for about an hour, in front of the only heater, to watch the parade. Then Jacqueline left to prepare for the ball that evening, and JFK started shaking hands. He seemed to enjoy himself enormously as the Cabinet, the ranking military, Supreme Court judges, and friends and relatives filed by to congratulate, to chat, to kid, to join in the fun.

I was standing about twenty feet behind him when he beckoned me to come over. I thought he meant someone in back of me, but he waved to me again. I went down, wondering what he had to tell me. He stuck out his hand and said, "How are you doing, Jacques?" I was so flustered I didn't know what to say. "Fine, Mr. President. It's a great day," I finally barely squeezed out. "I agree," he said. "It certainly is," and he turned back to the parade.

Then the PT–109 float came by, with members of his wartime crew on it. An enormous howl went forth now from this distinguished gathering. "Great work!" he exclaimed. From then on it was a party.

John F. Kennedy went around talking to all. "Are you getting any good shots today, Jacques?" he inquired of me later. And as the parade wore on the general spirit became more elated.

The parade—whose marshal was Lieutenant General James Gavin—featured 32,000 marchers, 86 bands (including drum majorettes who were frozen blue and twirlers whose batons seemed icy), the entire West Point Corps of Cadets and Annapolis Brigade of Midshipmen, plus jets, tanks, a 175-millimeter gun, missiles, horses, mules, and dogs. There was even a buffalo, ridden by a bearded Texan—which Kennedy enjoyed immensely. Also from Texas came the world's largest drum—part of the University of Texas' Longhorn Band.

From top: JFK,
Harry S. Truman,
Speaker of the House
Sam Rayburn.

From top: Eunice Kennedy Shriver,
Secretary of State
Dean Rusk,
Ambassador Joseph P. Kennedy.

Darkness was now falling. The last floats were straggling by. Guam, American Samoa, the Panama Canal Zone, were the last floats and the President, now flanked by his brothers, was there to the very end. Practically everybody else had left by now, but the last impression I have of that parade is John F. Kennedy and his brother, Robert, standing against the dark evening sky, saluting the last flag going by.

Darkness had fallen by 6:15 p.m., when the new President left the stand. I followed him into the White House for my first visit. The President had gone "home" and—until the Inaugural Balls reactivated Washington's social calendar—I was free to roam. I wandered through White House corridors, into Pierre Salinger's office, and was shown into the President's office. Standing there alone in the oval office that night, with its green carpet and its light walls, the seal, the two flags and the sailing pictures on the wall, I felt the sudden, delayed realization that the American people had chosen John Fitzgerald Kennedy to be their Chief Executive.

I couldn't help thinking that only twelve years before I had come to this country as an immigrant. My adopted land had been good to me and fulfilled many of its promises. But of all the opportunities granted me, the rarest had been to be a witness to and part of the emergence of a President.

The President left the last Inaugural party at 3 a.m. But the festivities were over now for quite a while. He had called a meeting of his staff for 9 a.m. that morning.

The New Frontier had started. Its work had begun.